The square of the hypotenuse

veni, vedi, vici

rhetoric
LOGIC

To Corinna, Ovid

ΡΤΟΛΜΙΣ

memo—BCE

# Manipulative Memos

Dear Mom,

Your pride in me
is one of the
greatest motivations
in my life.

Your son —

# Manipulative Memos

## Control Your Career through the Medium of the Memo

Arthur D. Rosenberg
Ellen Fuchs Thorn

TEN SPEED PRESS
Berkeley, California

1🕮

Ten Speed Press
P.O. Box 7123
Berkeley, CA 94707

The paper used in this publication meets the requirements
of the American National Standard for Permanence of Paper
for Printed Library Materials Z39.48–1984.

Library of Congress Cataloging-in-Publication Data

Rosenberg, Arthur D.
   Manipulative memos : control your career through the medium of the
memo / Arthur D. Rosenberg, Ellen Fuchs Thorn.
      p.    cm.
   Includes bibliographic references (p.    ) and index.
   ISBN 0-89815-614-9 : $18.95. — ISBN 0-89815-659-9 (pbk.) : $9.95
   1. Memorandums.    2 Office politics.    3. Manipulative behavior.
I. Thorn, Ellen Fuchs.    II  Title.
HF5733.M4R67    1994
658.4'53—dc20                                                94-27914
                                                             CIP

PRINTED IN THE UNITED STATES OF AMERICA

For Catherine
and
for Gerry

# Contents

# Preface

*You are going to be rich and famous, maybe.*

FORTUNE COOKIE

The fortune cookie that yielded the above message was traced to a bakery on Mott Street in New York City's Chinatown. Persistent research uncovered the writer, an English teacher and translator living in Pasadena, whose grandparents originated from the Beijing area. As best we could determine, the quote is the progeny of ancient wisdom and modern pragmatism, an unbeatable combination in our cosmopolitan society. Its meaning, open to some interpretation, brings us to the point that while nothing in life is absolutely certain, almost anything is possible.

The world is an increasingly complex place because of the growth of populations and the acceleration of information flowing along the expanding information highway. Approximately half the people ever born are alive today and many of those with whom you come in contact can affect your life. You deal with people of all kinds merely to survive, much less to get ahead, so it is reasonable to expect your relationship with each to vary. Some associations are agreeable, others unpleasant; some may be straightforward, others convoluted. Each relationship or interaction can be treated as an isolated environment subject to your control.

Like exercise videos and related products, manipulative memos (MM) can help you succeed if you use them. Success, however you define it, is unlikely to fall from the sky, a fortune cookie, or the pages of a book. We offer you concepts based on ancient wisdom and modern pragmatism, to control the environment in which you live and love.

*New York*                                                                A. D. R.
*September 1994*                                                      E. F. T.

# Acknowledgments

For their material and spiritual contributions, their encouragement, and their patience, we thank Howard Berelson, whose mural enfolds our memos; Phil Wood, Christine Carswell, Judith Dunham, and the staff at Ten Speed Press; and the friends and family who have graciously given their time and efforts in helping us more effectively manipulate our readers. Thank you, Ros Berlow, Chris Carr, Stu Cooper, Shelia Fischman, Marty Fuchs, John Lax, Jim Ozello, Zeil Rosenberg, Sig Rosenthal, Mike Rothstein, Andrea Spinelli, Jerry Stolls, Dave Stoner, Paul Walker, Rosemary Wellner, and Don Winkler.

# Manipulative Memos

# 1

# Introduction

*The people who get on in this world are the people who get up and look for the circumstances they want, and, if they can't find them, make them.*

GEORGE BERNARD SHAW

Many people believe that they have little or no control in shaping their own destiny. Some of us, however, are determined to mold our surroundings closer to our liking and to make the best of the environment in which we find ourselves.

When the playing field is level, people are treated fairly and ideas are presented and implemented or rejected on their merit alone. Perhaps you have a boss who values your input, an office manager who willingly provides the resources you need, and an accountant who shows you how your ideas can be made economical. Perhaps you are surrounded by loyal colleagues in a supportive atmosphere ideal for growth, creativity, and problem solving.

But the field isn't always level and success is not necessarily based on ability. We've all met brilliant, talented, and dedicated professionals who were working for people less intelligent, talented, or dedicated. Each successive stage up the corporate hierarchy requires less technical ability and more manipulative control: The Tellers design the bombs, the factory owners manufacture and sell them, and the politicians decide when and where to drop them.

We share the office arena with some people who assume home-field advantage as they strut about exuding confidence and reaching for whatever they may want. For all their swagger, however, many are intimidated or frustrated when they find themselves required to "put it in

1

writing." The written medium is one that equalizes the brash and the modest, the obtrusive and the shy, the aggressive and the diffident. Practiced pose and oratory hold no advantage on this field. Quick wit falls short to thoughtful prose and carries little weight in decision making. Imposing gestures are less compelling than documented argument. By controlling the medium with a persuasive memo or report, you can tilt the playing field to your advantage.

Success in a competitive environment demands that you take control of your career to get credit for your work, recognition from management, and respect from your peers. To this end, we advocate the power of composed persuasion, of convincing someone to do what you wish or refrain from doing what you don't want.

Our purpose is to help you control your career through the medium of the memo—to show you how to use manipulative memos—and to enable you to recognize when someone else's memos are manipulating you. Many of the basic, defensive, and offensive concepts described in this book may already be familiar to you—and are widely used by others in your workplace—although you may not have considered just how helpful they can be.

# Defining Your Objective

*A problem well stated is a problem half solved.*

CHARLES F. KETTERING

Before you start to write, it is important to identify a specific objective. Without a clear purpose, your thoughts are apt to be unfocused and ineffective, causing you to miss important opportunities.

*Scenario:* Steve is the head of Customer Service. His position is equivalent to Ingrid's, who is in charge of Manufacturing. Both report to Igor, who sends out this memo.

> To:     Staff
> From:   Igor
> Re:     Production Committee Meeting
> Can you make the above on Tuesday at 10?

Steve might respond in several ways.

 To:  Igor
From:  Steve

The Production Committee meeting date is okay with me.

To:  Igor
From:  Steve

Cannot make the Production Committee meeting on Tuesday—
how about Wednesday?

Although marginally sufficient, neither of these responses promotes the goals of Steve or his department. If he were having ongoing problems with Manufacturing, Steve could determine that the primary goal of his memo should be to seek an advantage over his competitor, Ingrid.

To:  Igor
From:  Steve

The Production Committee date is fine.
　　I'm also attaching this week's status report for my department FYI. The problems are highlighted, and came about due to the lack of scheduling information from Manufacturing.

If his problems with Manufacturing were only occasional, Steve might try another strategy with a pair of memos, with the first going to Igor.

To:  Igor
From:  Steve

The Production Committee date is fine. The departmental status report is attached FYI.

With the second memo, Steve pursues a more cordial working relationship with his counterpart, Ingrid.

To:  Ingrid
From:  Steve

I sent Igor this week's status report in preparation for the Production Committee meeting (copy attached).
　　As you can see, there are a couple of holes due to lack of schedule information. Can we get together at 9 on Tuesday to solve these problems before the Production Committee meets?

With a clear purpose in mind, it is easy to target whom you must influence. When Steve intended to attack Ingrid, he targeted his memo at Igor—the one with power over Ingrid. When his goal was to resolve the problems, however, his target became Ingrid.

Your goals are bound to vary in different situations and over time. Are you trying to motivate or to inhibit action? Are you justifying what you've already done or what you plan to do? Are you trying to generate good feelings, support, or confusion? Do you wish to gain someone's confidence? Or are you looking for a larger office or higher salary?

Your strategy is shaped by who you are and whom you intend to manipulate. Colleagues are approached differently from strangers, bosses from subordinates, creditors from debtors, and allies from opponents. Sometimes delicate factors such as age, gender, ethnicity, or personal idiosyncrasies (e.g., a history of violence) come into play.

Base your approach on your personal inclinations and on the paths available within your environment. This requires understanding the organization's culture, the formal and unwritten rules by which its games are played. Is there a single set of rules for everyone or different rules at different levels? In some companies, loyalty to your department is rewarded; in others, you must connive and politick to get ahead. In any environment, it is natural to strive to advance your career. But the course you choose must take into account the culture of your company.

> To:      Igor
> From:    Ingrid
> Re:      Scheduling
>
> Can we get together today at 4 on the above? I'll meet you at the *Malt and Brew.*

Meetings like this are arranged every day. Yet Ingrid's well-intentioned memo would be counterproductive if, for example:

- Ingrid's scheduling goal requires reams of computer printouts to be spread out on small bistro tables.
- Igor's boss disapproves of off-site meetings during business hours.
- Igor is weak in scheduling.
- The corporation does not condone drinking of alcohol.
- Igor is a notorious womanizer.

# Game Plan

*The will to win is not nearly as important as the will to prepare to win.*

BOBBY KNIGHT

With your objective and target in mind, you might opt for a *verbal* implementation of your plan—why abandon your advantage if you play well to an audience? However, written communication has its own advantages: body language and appearance play no role, there is no fumbling for words, you have time to prepare your best presentation, and you alone control the pace and content.

Written communications may vary in length from a single word to volumes, in any format. They can be recorded on memo pads, sticky flags, stationery, scrap paper, or greeting cards, or can be sent electronically through E-mail or fax. Successful businesses today are more attuned to function than to "correct" form, and E-mail commonly dispenses with all but the bare essentials. While reflecting a modern flexibility, this book reminds its readers that even the most informal notes can carry powerful and timeless messages by introducing some enduring tactics.

We define memos as any written or electronic communication. We provide short examples and longer scenarios throughout *Manipulative Memos (MM)* to show that presentation can be as important as content in reaching your goal. We support our points with current (real and imagined) and historic examples and suggest alternative approaches and outcomes to enable you to choose those best suited to your need and style. When we include thumbs down choices, we compare them with more successful solutions.

All of the competitive areas of life—love, war, sports, and work—have three interrelated parts: basic skills, defense, and offense. No matter how good your offense, most experts agree that you cannot win without a solid defense, and you can't get anywhere without a firm grasp of the basics. *MM* begins by introducing The Basics to prepare you to play with the professionals. In the first part, we identify and organize these resources in a way that can be applied to both defense and offense.

Written forms of personal criticism appear each day throughout the cubicles, corridors, and computers of corporate America. Although they are  less violent than face-to-face encounters, the successful office dweller has to defend against these threats. When attacked, you must be prepared to defend both your person and your position. It is also helpful to know how to carry through a preemptive strike against a possible future attack. *Manipulative Memos* provides you with the means to defend against attack (regardless of its validity) and to preempt attacks before they materialize.

In the final part of the book, devoted to offense, we describe how to take control by initiating action instead of sitting back and waiting to react.

The perfect game plan is made up of a balance of these basic, defensive, and offensive skills. Proper balance depends on the circumstances of the game and the identity of all the players. Are the contending factions evenly matched? Is it a team or one-on-one contest? A single round or entire match? What are the stakes? What resources are available? With all this in mind, *MM* shows you how to assess the circumstances, choose your tactics, and position yourself or your team to win.

# The Basics

Re:

The Basics are the pervasive skills we need to pursue our desired goals. Whether to protect what we already have or acquire something we want, timing, numbers, leverage, camouflage, and other tools are likely to come into play.

# 2

# Interpreting Truth

*Thrusting my nose firmly between his teeth, I threw him
heavily to the ground on top of me.*

MARK TWAIN

We're taught to think of truth as absolute, as though there were one reality shared by us all. Experience proves otherwise, for well-intentioned
people have been known to disagree. To control an area of contention,
you may need to influence the way others view a situation.

Our observations are influenced by personal perceptions and objec-
tives, so each of us sees reality from a somewhat different perspective.
If you ask a tennis player, beaten by a slightly better player, how he
played, he'll assure you that his game was off. Ask an insurance agent
to make good on a loss, and you may find that your policy didn't cover
what you thought it did. Here is a note with a decidedly self-serving
point of view.

> Dear Homeowner,
>
> We regret to inform you that the collapse of your home during the
> recent upheaval is not covered by your earthquake insurance. The
> policy clearly states that the insurer cannot be held responsible for
> such construction flaws as those which evidently led to this
> unfortunate but unrelated incident.
>
> On the brighter side, be sure to send for your free copy of our
> "Survive It Somehow" manual, complete with updated sections on
> hurricanes, tsunamis, computer viruses, recession, shark bite, and
> aging-realization syndrome.
>
> —F. Duckout, Licensed Broker

As you prepare to write your next memo, remember that your version of truth may not be shared. You may need to orient your memo toward helping others see things your way.

*Scenario:* Burt was supposed to complete a report by April 30. Unfortunately, he was in bed with the flu the last week of April and wasn't able to finish the report until the following week. He sends the report to his boss, Arnold, with an accompanying note.

>  To:      Arnold
> From:   Burt
>
> The report you asked me to finish by April 30 is attached. Sorry it is over a week late, but as you know, I was out with the flu for a week.

Instead of apologizing for being late, Burt would be better off writing a memo that casts himself in a more favorable light.

> To:      Arnold
> From:   Burt
>
> Here is the report (attached). Despite my having been out with the flu, I've still managed to cover all the issues you requested.

*Scenario:* Evan's supervisor asks for comments on an extremely complex proposal. Overwhelmed by the report, Evan sends the following note:

> Lee—
>
> I don't understand your plan.
>
> —Evan

Instead of admitting a personal shortcoming, Evan could simply state the need for further clarification—for the benefit of other department members.

> Lee—
>
> Your plan is unclear to the less technical members of the department. It would be helpful to all concerned if you would elaborate on your proposed schedule and costs.
>
> —Evan

Alternatively, Evan could turn the blame back to the writer, although this approach may not be the best when dealing with one's boss.

> Lee—
>
> Your plan is puzzling.
>
> —Evan

# Accentuate the Positive

*The man who has no imagination has no wings.*
MUHAMMAD ALI

Truth is based on individual points of view. This allows you to emphasize the *positive* aspects of your unique perspective, by selecting the points you choose to make and the clarity you use to express them.

## Selective Inclusion

The details you include—or avoid—contribute to your version of the truth. Enhance the facts to your advantage, but be careful to avoid verifiable falsehoods. It is essential not to produce written evidence that may be used against you. Instead, spiff up your account of real-life events. In each of these contrasting pairs, subjective truth is promoted by selecting points likely to appeal to the target audience.

👎 She was a housewife in a six-person household.

👍 She managed and organized a six-member institution with an annual budget of over $65,000.

👎 He represented the losing gubernatorial candidate.

👍 He organized and coordinated the political campaign for a major gubernatorial candidate.

👎 Our organization trained six lion tamers, only one of whom was eaten.

👍 Our organization trained six lion tamers, five of whom continue to excel.
Rosenberg, pp. 35–36

*Scenario:* Rick wants the larger cubicle due him and knows that there is one now available, but he realizes that the office manager, Mr. Bullhead, isn't likely to accommodate him if he just asks for it. Rick draws on an old sports injury, calls his doctor, and complains of a pain in his left knee. The doctor says he may have a little arthritis, recommends aspirin, and tells Rick to keep off it when it hurts. Rick shows up the following morning wearing a knee brace and tells everyone that he needs room to stretch his leg.

Next, Rick convinces Ms. Sickley, the employee compensation supervisor, to agree in principle that he'd be better off in a larger workspace and politely asks her to inform Mr. Bullhead. If she does so, he's got the support he wants. If not, he will compose his own note to Bill Bullhead, citing Sickley.

> Bill—
>
> You're probably aware of my bad leg and the trouble it's been causing me in my little cube. Well, Ms. Sickley told me that a larger cubicle, like the one in the northeast corner that just became vacant, would allow me to stretch the leg and still get in a full day's work. Do you think that could be arranged? It would sure solve a lot of problems!
>
> —Rick

In his memo, Rick presents the positive aspects of his case for obtaining the larger cubicle. In the unlikely event that Bullhead and Rick's supervisor compare notes, Rick is covered by his conversation with Ms. Sickley and his visit to the doctor. If all this seems a lot of trouble, consider how badly Rick wants the larger cubicle.

## Clarity

> *I never give them hell. I just tell the truth, and they think it's hell.*
>
> HARRY TRUMAN

Many of us conceal our intentions by not stating them clearly and then curse the world for failing to understand. Knowing what you want to express doesn't guarantee that others will understand what you say or write. And if you're not entirely certain about what you wish to make known, you're in for a long day.

Begin by defining your objective. Then determine the best way to achieve it. Finally, write so that your target will be able follow your train of thought: concisely, to the point, and with your "big guns" in a prominent position.

> A number of people have shown concern about the promotional plans and marketing strategies that may be developed soon. For instance, one person inquired if we were indeed planning to use the marketing channel of newspaper and journal advertising for the upcoming campaign for the *Widget*. Our chairman is also

concerned, in that he has told his golfing buddies that it would be
advertised in this week's paper.

In the above memo, the most powerful factor (the Chairman's interest)
is not mentioned until the last sentence of a long paragraph. A more
effective memo would place this tool in a more prominent position.

 The Chairman deems it essential to advertise our *Widget* in *this*
*week's paper.*
Please comment so that I can report to him.

*Scenario:* The *New York Times* carried a portion of a message sent by
George M. Steinbrenner III to other major league baseball club owners.
It seemed to be an appeal for them to join with him against baseball commissioner Faye Vincent.

> . . . It is very difficult for me to write this letter to you and the other
> owners. I hope you will believe me when I tell you that I have tried
> my level best to bring about a desirable conclusion to a matter
> which has plagued me and severely damaged the Yankee Partner
> ship as well as seriously affected my family, not only materially, but
> also mentally and physically.
> It is an ordeal that I hope no other owner in baseball will ever
> have to endure. It has been repugnant and distressing to think that
> what has happened to me could actually happen in this nation of
> ours without regard to the laws of the land and the justice system
> under which we live.
> I have enclosed two self-explanatory letters. One, a final plea
> with the Commissioner to meet with me, which as you see was
> summarily turned down. I find myself left with no alternative but to
> protect my family, myself and the Partnership of which I was chosen
> General Partner. I hope you will understand that I tried. 3/25/92

According to the *Times,* the memo made little impression on the people
who received it. Steinbrenner could have written more clearly to gain the
support of his peers.

> I am writing to you regarding the Yankee Partnership's conflict
> with the Commissioner's office. The outcome of this situation will
> establish precedents for all of us in the future.
> I have enclosed a copy of my request to the Commissioner to
> meet with me and a copy of his refusal.

> It is time for us to confront this serious challenge to our
> legitimate interests.  I will call next Monday to ask for your
> agreement.

Despite our reservations on Mr. Steinbrenner's writing style, it's only fair to note that Vincent *was* later removed as commissioner.

When pressed to do something against your wishes, clarity verging on bluntness can be effective.

*Scenario:* Hector's office is planning a party over the Memorial Day weekend, but the cost is beyond his means.  An obnoxious colleague, who would like to embarrass him, leaves an application for the trip on his desk with the following memo.

> Hector—
> The deposit for the Bimini trip is due tomorrow.
>    Is there some reason why you aren't planning to join us?
> —Tony

Hector's reply is clear and to the point.

> Tony—
> As you know, I cannot afford to make the trip.
> —Hector

This abrupt response offers Tony no room for maneuvering.  Since Hector's situation is already known, Tony will get no mileage by showing it to anyone.  If he does wave it around, they're more likely to react with respect for Hector and distaste for Tony.

# Eliminate the Negative

*I have received memos so filled with managerial babble
that they struck me as the literary equivalent of assault
with a deadly weapon.*

PETER BAIDA

In presenting your standpoint, you don't need to include the negatives— your opponents will be more than willing to do this for you.  When there are definite drawbacks to your position, consider a trio of alternate strategies:  selective omission, intentional ambiguity, and excuses.

## Selective Omission

*The withholding of truth is a major strategy of power.*

JOHN AND BOGDANA CARPENTER

A resumé mentioned earlier promoted the fact that an organization trained lion tamers and that 84 percent continued to excel in the field. It omitted highlighting the 16 percent who were less fortunate. In promoting your point of view, it is often preferable to omit conflicting details.

 In order to fulfill my travel obligations, I need an additional $2,000 in T&E funding.
This travel is necessary to get my sales into the black (and overcome the $100,000 deficit).

 I have excellent sales prospects on the West Coast that could result in nearly $100,000 in additional sales.
I need your approval for this trip, which will cost $1,800. Details and budget are attached.

*Scenario:* Johansson, vice president of sales, mentions to the eastern regional sales manager that all travel will probably be stopped through July 1. It's not definite, however, and he'll decide in three weeks, by the first of April.

Jealous of the impressive figures generated by the western region, the eastern regional sales manager decides to wrest a profit from the probable upcoming moratorium on travel. He instructs his staff to squeeze in all possible travel prior to April 1 and sends the following E-mail to the western regional sales manager.

> Johansson told me that he expects all travel to be curtailed through July 1.

If the western regional sales manager assumes the moratorium is definite, the eastern region can gain a month's advantage on the western region.

*Scenario:* Hugh finds out about the moratorium and writes to his boss, Arnold:

> Mr. Johansson has instructed that all business travel be completed before April 1. That means I'll have to schedule my trip to Boston for next week—O.K.?

## Ambiguity

> *Bud [McFarlane] was routinely mocked for his*
> *impenetrable prose and obfuscation, a circuitous dialect*
> *that was affectionately known as "McFarlanese," that*
> *was deemed evasive even by the standards of diplomacy.*

OLIVER NORTH

The opposite of clarity is ambiguity, often a convenient way to cloud an issue, especially a weakness in your position. Phrases that on the surface seem reasonable or promising can obscure the truth. These are examples of what we call "don't hold your breath" language.

- I'll get back to you.
- It's under consideration.
- Let me sleep on it.
- As soon as possible.
- I can make widgets or schedules.
- Don't expect miracles.
- The check is in the mail.

Other stock phrases are used to play down negative results.

- Slightly behind schedule.
- Minor difficulties.
- Results were inconclusive.
- Modest cost overrun.
- Within allowable limits.
- What would be your second choice?
- We'll do the best we can.

Masters of manipulation draw you into their confidence to get you to commit yourself. Here are some examples of "deja vu all over again":

- Off the record.
- I won't hold you to it.
- Just give me a ballpark figure.

You can avoid committing yourself to a position or specific point of view—to hedge while sitting on the fence—by using words with multiple interpretations.

- I just read your remarkable report.
- Your facility with the topic astounds me.

Is *remarkable* a compliment or a criticism?  What about *astounds*?  We call these weasel words "mysterious modifiers."  Here are others with which you can begin to build your own collection.

| | | |
|---|---|---|
| amazing | incredible | seductive |
| astonishing | interesting | slick |
| curious | memorable | unbelievable |
| explosive | revealing | unreal |

This letter of reference, from an anonymous writer, is a masterpiece of ambiguity.

> To Whom It May Concern:
>
> I am pleased to say that this is a former colleague of mine.  In my opinion you will be fortunate to get this individual to work for you. I recommend him with no qualifications whatsoever.
>
> No person would be better for the job.  I urge you to waste no time in making this candidate an offer of employment.  All in all, and without reservation, I cannot say enough good things about him, nor can I recommend him too highly.

If you're worried about the letter of recommendation that you may receive, supply your own letter for the signature.  Be sure to select carefully what you want included and omitted.

Phrases like "we regret" acknowledge an unpleasantness in an impersonal way that disavows responsibility.

> We regret that your check was lost in the mail.  This should not have happened.

Using passive language to distance yourself suggests impartiality and may obscure the action.  Instead of using the first person, you can remove yourself from the action and reduce your responsibility.

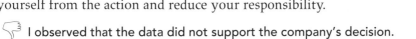 I observed that the data did not support the company's decision.

The data did not support the company's decision.

Observations of the data were made, and it was found that they did not support the company's decision.

The phrases *trust me* and *quite frankly* suggest that the remaining content may be suspect.  Words like *claimed, supposedly, so-called, reputed,* and *alleged* also raise doubts about the statements that follow.

- The claimed profitability of . . .
- Supposedly safe, . . .
- The so-called benefits of this product . . .

Other phrases can strengthen your contention:

- In our clearly successful first quarter . . .
- Undoubtedly, . . .
- I am pleased to confirm that . . .

*Scenario:*  Federal Reserve Board chairman Alan Greenspan was tagged "The Fed's Master of Obfuscation."  Pressured to cut interest rates to hasten economic recovery, Greenspan addressed the senators at a Congressional hearing.

> While I've indicated to you previously that we may well have, probably do have, enough monetary stimulation in the system to create that [economic recovery], I'm not sure that we will not need some insurance or to revisit this issue, and all I can say to you is that we're all looking at the same set of data, the same economy, the same sense of confidence which pervades it.  We're all making our judgments with respect to how that is evolving with respect to economic activity and where the risks of various different actions are.  And there will be differences inevitably.
>
> ("Washington Memo," New York Times, 4/20/92)

Vague or undefined terms, non sequiturs, false analogies, and undocumented assertions all have their place in the annals of ambiguity as they divert facts into someone's interpretation of truth.

## Excuses

> *The girl who can't dance says the band can't play.*
> YIDDISH PROVERB

Used to justify something that you didn't, won't, or cannot do adequately, excuses may get you off the hook, but most of the time they are viewed with suspicion.  Happily, there is a better way.  When replying to an embarrassing query, you can respond with candor, skillfully dodge a direct response, or use humor to diffuse the issue.

When you respond candidly, avoid admitting your ignorance.

👎 I'm not too well-informed on the subject.

👍 I'm in the process of reviewing the question in additional detail so that the report will be as thorough as possible.

👎 I didn't realize you needed the report so soon.

👍 If you needed the report today, you should have informed us of the schedule at least a week ago.

If this fails, you can try to evade the issue.

👎 Things have been so hectic lately.

👍 It's on the top of my to-do list.

👎 We're waiting for approval.

👍 Pending approval, we're exploring some viable alternatives.

A touch of humor may be preferable to a lame excuse.

👎 I got stuck in traffic/an elevator/a meeting.

👍 I got stuck in a pot of glue.

👎 I couldn't help it.

👍 I was attacked by a killer rabbit.

# Cover Memos

*The best-expressed interpretation will prevail more often than the truth.*

A cover memo is a "letter of introduction" for an attachment. It identifies the source of the attachment and may be used to direct your target's attention to a specific portion of its content. The cover memo is a unique opportunity for you to present truth as you see it: you can highlight and reword supportive points and steer your reader away from harmful ones.

👎 J. W.—
The XYZ report is attached for your information.
—J. B.

This kind of memo is a wasted opportunity, for it does no more than introduce an attachment. In the following example, Gloria makes better use of her cover memos.

*Scenario:* While promoting the in-house conversion of data disks, Gloria comes across a special report from American Data Retrieval (ADRCo), a major conversion house. The early portions of this report appear supportive of Gloria's position, although the latter sections go into great detail about the security and backup challenges.

👍 From:   Gloria
To:      Disk Committee
The attached ADRCo Special Report has excellent information on disk conversion—see pages 4–5.

Gloria highlights the material that supports her case, thereby accentuating the positive. Concerned that the committee members might find the report too technical and set it aside, she ensures that her points are made clearly by summarizing or rewording the content.

👍 From:   Gloria
To:      Disk Committee
The attached ADRCo Special Report makes four important points on disk conversion—pages 4–5:
1. Major companies do their own data conversion.
2. The equipment is relatively inexpensive.
3. A full-time professional should administer the process.
4. Benefits:  time, security, and flexibility.

Gloria uses a cover memo to present her points clearly and concisely. She did *not* refer to points that would be critical of her recommendations— why encourage the decision makers to read further?

 If the critical arguments are too obvious to ignore, she might bring them up and weaken them while appearing fair and unbiased.

👍 From:   Gloria
To:       Disk Committee

The attached ADRCo Special Report makes four important points on disk conversion—pages 4–5:

1. Major companies do their own data conversion.
2. The equipment is relatively inexpensive.
3. A full-time professional should administer the process.
4. Benefits:  time, security, and flexibility.

   On the flip side, the report also lists some potential problems on page 16.  It seems that all of them are surmountable if we set up a *professional* operation.  In other words, it is critical to use a full-time professional (point 3 above).

By acknowledging these problems, Gloria manages to use them to support one of her positions.

# 3

# Timing

*There is a time to let things happen and a time to make things happen.*

HUGH PRATHER

Timing is an important factor in controlling your environment. Like truth, timing requires careful judgment, and inappropriate decisions can be fatal. Even after years of driving, when merging into highway traffic becomes automatic, it still demands accurate timing. As well as judging *your* speed and position, you must judge that of the *other* driver.

Opportunities are gained and lost by recognizing—or failing to recognize—when to act or pause. A timely memo can work wonders, while failure to act at the right moment can hurt your cause.

*Scenario:* As the infamous Mata Hari awaited execution by firing squad near Paris, she appealed to the Dutch government to intervene on her behalf. Unaware of the severity of her plight until too late, she lost her last opportunity for a reprieve.

> To:     Dutch Government Officials
> From:   Margaretha G. Zelle [alias Mata Hari]
>
> Jealously—vengeance—there are so many things that crop up in the life of a woman like me, once people know that she finds herself in a difficult position.

In this situation, the Mata Hari should have more accurately read her jailers' clock and changed the timing of her letter. Alternatively, she might have written a different letter aimed at delaying her scheduled execution. These two options—telling time and resetting the other person's clock—are the focus of this chapter.

# Telling Time

*I wasted time, and now doth time waste me.*

SHAKESPEARE

In the office, successful timing requires you to be aware of your own schedules and deadlines, and to read the priorities and clocks of those around you. Your boss is more inclined to let you take on additional responsibility when her administrative assistant quits. On the other hand, you're unlikely to be granted a salary increase the same month you mess up an important presentation.

The first priority is clearing your own clock so that you can accurately read your target's. Set aside enough time to cool down, review, and evaluate your options when you are upset or uncertain about how to proceed. This is especially critical when using E-mail, which often tempts the writer into immediate, and sometimes counterproductive, action.

When times are good and funds are plentiful, your target may be open to new ideas. Read your target's clock to time your move.

> I'm sure you share my enthusiasm about this quarter's sales and are concerned about what we can do for an encore.
> To maintain the momentum you have established, I would like to offer a proposal.

Conversely, your target may be basking in the glow of these good times and unwilling to risk a change. In this case, a more forceful approach may be justified.

> I imagine that you're rightly pleased with this quarter's sales. However, we must reinvest a percentage of these profits to maintain the momentum that you have established. (Remember General Motors in the 1970s—they gloried in their profits and neglected to reinvest in the market, with disastrous results that are felt even today.)
> As reinvestment is critical, I propose that we take the following action.

Bad times also influence priorities. When battered by adversity, people may waffle between conservative and daring. Managers may be responsive to new ideas when times are so awful that they are inclined to grasp at straws, or they may cling to old standbys. Decision makers who are about to retire may want to avoid unnecessary risk or they may want to take one last glorious gamble. There are no fixed rules.

Deadlines for budget projections are taken very seriously, and managers have been known to lose out on funding because of inadequate timing. If someone else is developing a budget that will affect your operation, call your needs to attention early in the process. There's no benefit in crying after the fact.

> This may be premature as the new budget is in the early planning stages, but I want to confirm our plans for the computer upgrades.
> I am attaching our cost projections for your reference.

Good timing may protect a portion of diminished funding before it disappears entirely.

> B. B.—
>
> I would like to carry forward the remaining budget allocated for union negotiations.
> We anticipate an increase in related activities toward the end of the fiscal year and will need the budgeted funds at that time.
> —J. W.

Fridays and the days preceding holidays tend to be periods of either reduced motivation (anticipating time off) or high tension (anxiety over clearing the desk before leaving). In either case, your target will be reluctant to embark on new ideas or projects. If you must send a memo on a topic you would prefer to duck, try to have it arrive on a Friday before a long weekend.

People need time to get back into their routine when they return to the office after an absence and may not entertain new ideas at such times. Memos are generally read most attentively Tuesday through Thursday. A solid proposal that you want seriously considered should reach your target Tuesday morning.

Another timing technique is to seek approval for a questionable aspect of a proposal at the eleventh hour. By waiting until it's too late for your boss to amend or alter your report, you may succeed in getting the whole plan approved.

> Mr. Flexor—
>
> Attached is my quarterly budget update. You can understand my satisfaction with the bottom line.
> Because we are currently below the corporate average, I allowed for an 8 percent salary increase for the staff, which will go a long way in maintaining the productiveness of our group.
> —Arnold Papadoupoulos

If Flexor reads this memo just before he leaves for the budget review, he may take it with him as a silver bullet for the review committee.

Some self-important executives claim they are too busy to read beyond the opening paragraph of a report or memo, so begin your report with a short paragraph summarizing your key points. Your objective will be met even if your target reads no further.

To:     Ms. Finch
From:  Hugh

This is the report you asked for on the negotiations with the Hamsters Union.

[the memo continues directly into the report]

This uninspired note does little to draw the reader into its context.

More effectively, Hugh could attach a separate cover note briefly summarizing the information Finch needs. This will promote Hugh's points and save Finch the time required to read the whole report.

To:     Ms. Finch
From:  Hugh
Re:     Attached Report on Negotiations with Hamsters Union

Please note the personal background of Walter Ruthless on page 23 (highlighted). Among other things, he has been brought up twice on union charges of conflict of interest with other companies in union negotiations.
    This certainly provides an insight into his "hot button."

### Contents
- page 1—Historical perspective (provides useful insights on their current position);
- page 16—Personal background on the chief negotiators; and
- page 27—Issue-oriented challenges relevant to our upcoming negotiations.

# Resetting a Clock

*You can't turn back the clock. But you can wind it up again.*

BONNIE PRUDDEN

Your success with timing may be determined by how well you read the mind of the person in the driver's seat. Recognize the need to match your priorities to those of others in the organization—not only your current superiors but also colleagues who someday may rise to that position. A timely response to a question is always appreciated; a delayed reply can lead to frustration and resentment. If your boss's request is not met on or before the time set on *his* clock, he is likely to see you as unreliable.

Once you have read your target's clock, you may want to reset it to be more in line with your priorities. If you sense that your boss's alarm is about to ring, try to reset his clock.

> Don Flexor—
>
> I have to delay the budget report as I am getting revised costs on union negotiations.
>     I will refine these numbers and get back to you on the 15th.
>
> —Hugh

It may be possible to postpone a meeting for which you are not yet prepared, or to offer an alternative.

> J. W.—
>
> Since the next Steering Committee meeting is scheduled prior to the release of the budget updates, it might be best for me to postpone my presentation until the following meeting.
>     Meanwhile, I'll be able to focus on the productivity report you asked me to work on.
>     I'll see that my presentation is removed from the current agenda before your assistant distributes it.
>
> —Arnold

If you and a colleague have similar goals, combine your efforts and double-team your target with separate but coordinated petitions that cannot be ignored.

*Scenario:* Felicia and Hugh still use typewriters, but want their company to purchase computers. One day, the carriage of Hugh's typewriter jars loose. Shortly thereafter, a key on Felicia's machine breaks and cuts her finger. The repair service is called, and a purchase order for an astronomical amount is issued.

Recalling a magazine article that stresses the safety and productivity of computers, Hugh and Felicia decide to double-team Arnold, their boss. Felicia bandages her finger and bursts into Arnold's office to tell him that she is going to the doctor. Hugh calls a friend who sells computers and leaves a handwritten note for Arnold.

> A—
>
> Felicia called. She'll be fine.
> > This month's status report may be late.
> Depends on when it can be typed.
> > Thought you'd find the attached article on
> computers and productivity interesting.
>
> —H

When the computer salesperson phones later in the day, Arnold is ready to act.

When you complete a task before its due date, consider holding it back until you can get more mileage from your work. Submitting a report before the deadline makes the task appear too easy. Holding it back is an insurance policy to be cashed in when you want to redirect a complaint or ask for a favor.

*Scenario:* Jean, in sales, has several accounts ready to sign on the dotted line. Initially Jean holds back because the end of the fiscal year is approaching and these new accounts will be a great start for the new year. But when Jean learns that the division has not met its annual quota, an MM to the division head saves the day—and year.

> To:    Vic
> From:  Jean
>
> You'll be pleased, I'm sure, to countersign the two attached contracts which will push the division over the top.
> > While your pen is handy, please also approve the one-week *Personal Leave Form* also attached.
> > Congratulation for getting your group on the Top Ten list.

A similar negotiating opportunity may occur when a colleague is on a tight time schedule and you have the power to delay him or speed him on his way. Being sensitive to his time frame, you can help him out while asking for something in return. This quid pro quo may simply be an off-hand comment that "you owe me" or a request for a more substantial concession.

# 4

# Using Numbers

*As long as I count the votes, what are you going to do about it?*

WILLIAM (BOSS) TWEED

Numbers have the power to impress and convince people, and can make your ideas and products seem more worthwhile than someone else's. Numbers can distort or dramatize, suggest, support, overwhelm, confuse, or implicate. Used effectively, numbers are hard to refute.

Because the intention of using numbers in a business memo is usually to inform and influence, not to mystify or awe, you do not have to be a mathematician to use numbers effectively—you want to use numbers that are comprehensible to your target.

👎 Our customers are in the top quartile with a standard deviation of .145 and a modal income of $153,200.

👍 Our customers are very well-off, with an average income of $153,200.

Just as you shape your version of the truth, you can always find numbers to support your point of view. These may be measurements which reflect the real world, like dollars or widgets, or *derived* numbers such as averages, percentages, and ratios, which compare one measurement to another.

This chapter will help you select the measurements and derived numbers that hook your audience into sharing—and accepting—your perspective.

# Measurements

*Never let your data get in the way of your analysis.*

THEODORE J. LOWI

The most commonly used numbers in business measure discrete items: dollars, hours, or units of a product.

Expenses were $945,000.

The total time spent was 245 hours.

Last year, sales were 3,456,000 units.

These examples do not indicate whether each measurement is good or bad. When someone boasts of $1 million in sales, this number could represent half of last year's figure, an increase of a mere .01 percent, or a fantastic performance compared with others in the company. Without contextual data, meaningful comparisons are limited.

To make the number more meaningful, you could add a verbal modifier to influence your reader.

Expenses were held down to $945,000.

Or you could provide a numerical context.

Expenses were $945,000 last year, as compared with $992,000 for the previous year.

Of the many measurements that may serve your purpose, select the alternative that best supports your argument. When reporting on expenses, for instance, you might want to stress the modest increase as opposed to the total figure.

Expenses are up only $3,000 over the previous year.

Time frame represents another variable that you can use to present numbers congenial to your purposes.

In the last quarter, expenses were less than the comparable period of the prior year.

Some managers even go so far as to use a departmental calendar that is different from the fiscal year of the company. Chosen with care, this departmental calendar will always provide good news when management typically asks for reassurance.

*Scenario:* The corporate officers at Zort Company often ask for information on inventory in October at the start of the company's calendar-year fourth quarter. Harold, the manager of inventory, is well aware of this tradition. However, because September is a hot season for marketing, inventory stocks must be high. He therefore has developed a departmental calendar different from Zort's fiscal year. Harold's calendar ends on August 1, before inventory climbs. When asked about inventory in October, Harold replies:

> For the inventory year just ended, we set a new company record for minimizing inventory costs.

In spite of its deviance from the Zort fiscal year, Harold's report is accepted because it is good news, because management can't get the needed information from anyone else, and because no one has raw data for a comparable period against which to check Harold's figures.

There is a trade-off between using exact numbers and using approximations. Precise measurements are impressive, but they draw attention to themselves and away from any other point you may want to make. Rounded numbers draw less attention to themselves and allow the reader to focus elsewhere.

If you want to direct your target to the cost of equipment, for example, use exact measurements.

👎 This equipment will cost less than $10,000.

👍 This equipment will cost only $9,564.

If you do not want to draw attention to the costs, use rounded measurements.

👎 This equipment will cost only $9,564.

👍 This equipment will cost less than $10,000.

You might mix rounded and exact measurements to persuade your reader to concentrate on savings rather than spending.

> This proposal, costing less than $10,000, will save $93,246 in only 90 days.

One situation where you should always use numbers that *appear* exact is in reporting expenses to your company or the IRS. An expense account item of $100 exactly will automatically be questioned, while the same item costing $114.32 will probably be accepted.

# Derived Numbers

*Never show card tricks to those you play poker with.*

HUGH SHARIF

When you cannot find an actual measurement to serve you, derive your own. Derived numbers are useful when measurements don't suit your purpose or you want to compare two measurements. Derived numbers commonly found in business include averages, percentages, and ratios.

> The average life of a receivable is 32 days.

> Expense as a percent of sales is 8 percent.

> The ratio of telemarketing phone calls per sale is 12:1.

Because people generally don't look behind your calculations to the original data, you can use them to lead your target in the direction of your choice. If actual measurements are not useful or impressive, or your sample is small, you can hide the limitation: 1 out of 10 and 100 out of 1,000 are both 10 percent or 1:10, and no one will ask about your sample size.

Derived numbers may benefit by including a *verbal* context by which you lead your reader.

> Expense as a percent of sales is only 8 percent.

> Unit costs have been reduced to $3.00 per widget.

You can use a *number* for comparison as well. The following examples all relate to the same basic numbers, but two are less impressive than the third—assuming that you wish to stress expense reduction.

 Expense as a percent of sales is 8 percent, down from last year's 9 percent.

Expense as a percent of sales is only 8 percent, down 1 percent from last year.

Expenses were reduced from last year by 11 percent, and are only 8 percent of net sales.

As with measurements, you can also manipulate the time frame from which your numbers are derived.

Expense as a percent of sales over the last three months has been cut by 3 percent.

Exact figures suggest precision in what might otherwise appear to be a guess. If you write 50 percent, people assume you rounded off the actual amount; 47.8 percent suggests that your numbers are precise (and, therefore, so is your logic). Avoid decimals like 33.3 and 66.7, for they are recognizable as one-third and two-thirds, which appear much like rounded numbers. If your percent is a whole number, express it to at least one decimal place (e.g., 45.0 percent rather than just 45 percent).

 The average of about 13 months . . .

 The average of 12.7 months . . .

 With an increase of about 20 percent . . .

 With an increase of only 17.8 percent . . .

There may be times when you do not want to be precise. For instance, if you were asked about expenses and they had risen to 12.5 percent, you could use whole numbers and make your response appear impromptu.

 Expenses continue to be maintained at around 10 percent with some seasonal fluctuation.

## Averages

*Everyone wants to be equal; no one wants to be average.*

RHUTRA

Average is how statisticians see the world. Above average is how most of us see ourselves. Below average is the way those of us who see ourselves as above average see nearly everybody else.

There are three types of average: mean, median, and mode. The mean is the arithmetic average (total the scores and divide by the number of scores). The median is the middle position (arrange the group of scores in ascending order and find the score in the middle). The mode is the score that occurs most often.

*Scenario:* Felicia, Burt, Hugh, Arnold, and J. W. earn $35,000, $35,000, $45,000, $50,000, and $85,000. The total payroll is $250,000. The mean is $50,000, the median is $45,000, and the mode is $35,000. Using the *mode*, B. B. O'Boile can claim to each employee:

Your salary is at or above the average.

Likewise, four of the five employees can accurately counter:

I am earning at or below the mean average.

The easiest way to diddle the computation of averages is by setting up categories and a time frame and then analyzing them. Garrison Keillor, when he says "And all the children are above average," uses the children of one population and the norms of another.

Sometimes you don't want to use the average figure. If you were asked about the total cost of insurance for your company, you might not want to say that the total costs had risen by an average of 20 percent in six months. Instead, you might break this figure down and show that the real culprit was medical insurance, a factor beyond your control.

The company cost for insurance over the last six months has risen by over 20% due to the runaway prices of medical insurance:
Liability: 2.3%
Compensation: 3.1%
Medical: 34.3%

*Scenario:* The personnel records in the company where Nelson works show that its salespeople were, on average, promoted to account executives within fourteen months of being hired. Nelson discovers that the three newest salespeople (all of whom he hired) had been promoted in 15, 14, and 9 months. He sends a note to his supervisor.

To:     Clarence
From:  Nelson
Sales training has shown a marked improvement, with the average promotion time decreasing from 14 to 12.7 months.

The numbers themselves don't tell the whole story. They omit the edict from on high that he needed to promote another female to account executive to keep Personnel happy, that his sister-in-law was pressuring him for a promotion for her son, that a sudden opening appeared when someone went on family leave, or that his own performance record—as a successful manager—benefits when he promotes subordinates.

## Percentages

> *Do not put your faith in what statistics say until you*
> *have carefully considered what they do not say.*

WILLIAM W. WATT

A percentage is obtained by dividing one measurement by another. To support your goal, search for the right combination of measurements.

Suppose you want to impress an audience with the company's profitability, but the profit for the most recent year was only $20,000 (2%) on $1 million sales. For the prior year, profit was $18,000 (also 2%) on sales of $900,000.

👎 Profits increased by $2,000.

👎 Profit was 2 percent of net sales.

👍 Profits increased 11 percent over last year.

*Scenario:* Stu is the head of Production. A directive comes down from Finance stating that the current year's Marketing and Production budgets will have to be reduced by a total of $25,000. Stu is already operating right on budget, and cutbacks are likely to result in production delays that may make him look bad next year. He feels the problem is largely Marketing's entertainment budget.

Marketing's annual budget of $400,000 is depleted heavily in the first quarter of the fiscal year when advertising space is purchased, and Production operates with $200,000 of expenses spread evenly throughout the year. The result is that each department is now left with only $50,000, from which the required $25,000 savings must come. Stu has no intention of sacrificing $12,500 from his budget and is determined to reduce his contribution.

> To:     Ros, Marketing
> From:   Stu, Production
>
> Regarding the $25,000 budget reduction, I feel that our two departments should share the cuts equally.

> I'm certain you will agree that this is equitable, and I will
> authorize the debits unless I hear from you by Friday.

When Friday arrives, he sends a memo to Finance.

> To: Imogene, Finance Department
> From: Stu, Production
> Re: $25,000 budget reduction
>
> As the proposed cut is 8⅓ percent of the combined annual budgets
> for Marketing and Production, please allocate 8⅓ percent equally
> against each of our departments:
>
> 8⅓% of $400,000 = $16,667 against Marketing
>
> 8⅓% of $200,000 = $8,333 against Production

In the first memo, Stu offers to share the cut equally, so Marketing
probably assumed that both departments would contribute equal *dollars.*
However, under Stu's guidance, Finance reduced the budgets by an equal
*percentage* of the annual budget, with two thirds of the $25,000 being
charged to Marketing. The charges against Production, which Stu feared
would be $12,500, were only $8,333.

One especially useful aspect of percentages is that they can be used
for either side of the argument: the glass is 47 percent empty or the
glass is 53 percent full.

*Scenario:* Charlie, one of the six people in an office, complains to Lee, the
office manager, about working conditions. Lee could respond by using
percentages advantageously.

> To: Charlie
> From: Lee
>
> Eighty-three percent of the people are satisfied with my leadership
> of the office.

On the other hand, Charlie could present the same percentages from
his perspective.

> To: Lee
> From: Charlie
>
> Nearly 20 percent of the employees are unhappy with the company.

When hard times strike, Lee offers Charlie and his five colleagues an
option: a temporary three-day work week with a salary cut of 50 percent

and a promise of a corresponding 50 percent increase when sales improve. The alternative is that the office will close and everyone will be out of work. They take the cut and Charlie's $500 salary becomes $250.

A few weeks later, the office returns to a five-day work week. When Charlie's next paycheck arrives, instead of the original $500, his new gross is only $375. This is indeed an increase of 50 percent over the $250 salary, and Charlie learns that a decrease calculated on one base is not offset by an equal percentage of increase on a lower base.

## Ratios

*He uses statistics as a drunken man uses lamp posts—*
*for support rather than for illumination.*

ANDREW LANG

Ratios are derived by comparing different units of measure, for example, miles per gallon or sales per telemarketer. As with percentages, select the measurements that can help you make your point.

*Scenario:* In a department of 36 members, 2 of the 4 managers and 16 of the support staff extend their lunch hour. Lee, the office manager, wants to censure the support staff without drawing attention to the lateness of the managers, and circulates the following note.

To:      Staff
From:   Lee
Managers and support staff are equally at fault in returning late
from lunch.

To avoid the the appearance of criticizing management, Lee might rewrite the note, basing it on *actual* rather than *relative* numbers.

To:      Staff
From:   Lee
More support staff than managers return late from lunch.

*Scenario:* Dave runs a company cafeteria that advertises fish chowder made up of equal (50:50) amounts of fresh scallops and defrosted codfish at $1.49 per serving. Sounds reasonable, so Leslie orders a bowl and digs in. When Leslie asks the waiter where the scallops are, he assures Leslie confidently, "They're in there. For every codfish, we throw in a scallop. One for one, or fifty-fifty."

Dave used a ratio based on the *number* of fish and scallops while his customers thought in terms of *volume*. Dave selected the units of measure to manipulate his diners.

This strategy can work as well in an office environment. For instance, it is possible that only 2 of every 100 orders result in complaints, each of which demands an average of 2 hours to resolve. A critic in Operations might question the time-per-complaint ratio of 2:1 and wonder why it takes so long to solve a simple shipping problem.

The head of Customer Service can respond that the 4 hours of service time spent for every 100 orders is an excellent 4:100 ratio of Customer Service time-per-order.

# Cause and Effect

*I always keep a supply of stimulant handy in case I see a snake—which I also keep handy.*

W. C. FIELDS

Two apparently unrelated events that occur sequentially are called a coincidence. When the sequence repeats often, people tend to assume a cause and effect relationship between the two events.

> Increasing the advertising budget will result in an increase of sales and therefore profit.

This tendency to assume a cause and effect relationship can be a powerful tool in shaping your memos. Note that we are talking not about a provable cause and effect relationship, but rather about the human tendency to connect two events in this way.

A memo may mislead your target into believing more than is really true. By writing the following memo, Smythe hopes that Alberti will assume that computerization is responsible for the reduction in overtime and total costs.

> To:     H. Alberti
> From:   R. F. Smythe
>
> Since the new computer system became operational on May 1, overtime charges have been reduced by 37 percent and total costs are 7.3 percent below budget.

When several explanations are available, it makes sense to pick the one that most closely matches your particular bias.

We regularly hear of implied cause and effect relationships.

> Cigarette smokers get lower grades in college than nonsmokers.

Does smoking cause lower grades? Do low grades make some students nervous, causing them to smoke? Do students with lower grades and those who smoke both take more study breaks? Or do instructors, jealous of students who can still afford to smoke, spitefully give them lower grades?

> Recent economic studies show that in industrialized nations, the gross national product (GNP) is in decline wherever lawyers outnumber doctors.

Is the predominance of lawyers a direct cause of the decline of the GNP, a byproduct, or merely a coincidence? Even if you were convinced that lawyers are an economic drain, the seeming rightness of the concept is not enough to justify the assumption of cause and effect. Nevertheless, you could still present the information and let your readers assume the connection. Only a sophisticated opponent would call your bluff.

# 5

# Leverage

*The appearance of power is power.*

LAURENCE J. PETER

Leverage means using power to get something done. In interpersonal relations, this power can be the force of your personality or the aura of a position. The politician in control of business zoning knows that the leverage he exerts over you will last only until your business permit has been approved. The bank can squeeze no longer once your debt is paid. A property owner may concede leverage to a trespasser with a gun. The promise of spousal attentions offers little leverage when desire has departed or alternatives arrived. Organization charts ignore the leverage factor because it is difficult to map and constantly in flux.

Leverage requires a light touch like that of the successful pickpocket in Calcutta who deftly pilfered wallets, withdrew only a modest portion of their contents, then returned the balance to their pockets of origin. When routinely stopped by the police, he always had a respectable sum of cash but never property that could be identified as stolen. No one ever leveled charges against him. Those who suspected something was amiss could never be completely certain they'd been robbed, or by how much.

## Personal Leverage

*If I only had a little humility, I'd be perfect.*

TED TURNER

Personal leverage is using your own reputation to get what you want. You are using personal leverage when you ask a favor of a friend or win a point based on your professional reputation. This is the leverage of choice by those whose record has earned them the respect of their colleagues and who have no positional leverage.

*Scenario:* Felicia, Burt, and Hugh report to Arnold, so that corporate hierarchy gives Arnold leverage over them. Arnold knows that Hugh is the fair-haired one and suspects he may someday be working under Hugh, so his leverage is somewhat mitigated.

Arnold is a bit old-world. Felicia, willing to use all advantages available to her, knows that she also has some leverage over Arnold.

Burt is little more than competent. To get ahead, he needs all the help he can get, especially from Arnold.

Felicia, well aware of her personal leverage, asks for a favor.

> To:      Arnold
> From:   Felicia
>
> I hate to ask you this, Arnold, but we're having weekend guests and I need to get home early on Friday to prepare for them.
>     I sure hope you don't mind if I leave around lunch and come in a bit late on Monday.
>     Thanks, I knew you'd understand.

She times her next MM in such a way that Burt has no opportunity to try to whine his way out. Burt either does what Felicia asks or risks disapproval from both Felicia and Arnold.

> To:      Burt
> From:   Felicia
>
> I need a big favor. I have to leave early this afternoon and I won't be able to finish reconciling my accounts on time. I've told Arnold that I trust you completely, so will you finish them up for me?
>     Thanks, Burt, I knew you'd help.

The problem with personal leverage is that it only extends so far. In any office, however, there will be a mix of other power. For instance, the corporate hierarchy gives Arnold *positional* leverage over Hugh, Felicia, and Burt. In addition, Arnold has breakfast most mornings in the company cafeteria with B. B. O'Boile, who is his boss's boss. This is really a matter of convenience, but Arnold's boss is intimidated by this breakfast dyad. Arnold could *borrow leverage* for his own use if he recognized his boss's insecurity.

# Positional Leverage

*If you do not immediately comply with my request,*
*I shall unfrock you, by God.*

ELIZABETH I

Positional leverage comes from your position in the corporate hierarchy. Most people will defer to a higher position, but with resentment. Pulling rank won't work on peers, and it will foster resentment from subordinates. One can easily guess the bishop's reaction, along with his compliance, to the following memo.

> To:     Dr. Richard Cox, Bishop of Ely
> From:   Queen Elizabeth [1573]
>
> Proud Prelate,
> You know what you were before I made you what you are now.  If you do not immediately comply with my request, I shall unfrock you, by God.                                 Brockway, p. 12

*Scenario:* Peter has been asked to arrange the schedule of an international visitor who is coming to his company's U.S. office.  Instead of calling his colleagues and asking for their cooperation, he issues the following memo.

> To:     Distribution listed below
> From:   Peter Wolf
>
> Johan Georges joined our international division last summer as a product manager.  He will be visiting the U.S. next week.
>     Please call my assistant, at extension 789, to set up a time when you can meet with Johan.

Are you surprised that no one called?  If Peter wanted cooperation, he shouldn't have placed himself above his peers ("call my assistant") or expected them to initiate the call.  It hardly matters if the memo was the product of arrogance, thoughtlessness, or naivete—what counts is that it failed in its intent.

When communicating with subordinates, it is important to be courteous and positive.  Get directly to the point.  Beating up on people is unproductive.  Overwhelming them can lead to confusion.

*Scenario:* Flexor needs a report by a certain date. His position is powerful enough to ensure his subordinate's cooperation.

> 👎 To:      Arnold Papadoupoulos
> From:    Don Flexor, Controller
> Re:       Your report entitled "Dyslexic Dividends"
> Date:     12/31/93
>
> Am I the only one around here who takes profitability seriously?
> I will expect a rewrite on my desk by 2/1/94, with a lot more
> substantiation in the way of graphs, charts, and statistics, and a sane
> title like "Department Dividends."

Flexor makes a point of reminding Arnold of his power. Arnold will do what the controller says, but with resentment and a little fear.

Arnold has to study the next example for quite a while to figure out what Flexor wants.

> 👎 To:      Arnold Papadoupoulos
> From:    Don Flexor, Controller
> Re:       Your report entitled "Dyslexic Dividends"
> Date:     12/31/93
>
> That was an interesting report on your division's profitability
> through the first two quarters of 1993, prorated through 1993 and
> compared to the figures of the past two years. Unfortunately, it will
> be necessary to undertake a revision, and to include some graphs,
> charts, and statistics to enhance the appearance and content of the
> report. It would be convenient for me to receive the report by
> 1/26/94, but absolutely no later than 2/1/94, in order to have its
> contents incorporated with the reports from other departments in
> time for the scheduled departmental reviews, which are likely to be
> scheduled some time in March. Not that some of us don't have a
> sense of humor, but you might change the title to something like
> "Departmental Dividends." As this is a matter of some urgency, I
> would very much appreciate your immediate attention to it.

Flexor's name and reputation are sufficient to ensure that Arnold will jump to his suggestions.

The following directive is more pleasant and encouraging than a heavy-handed approach and is predictably more effective. The word *appreciate* softens the tone.

To:      Arnold Papadoupoulos
From:    Don Flexor
Re:      Your report on "Dyslexic Dividends"
Date:    12/31/93

Please rewrite to include some more substantiation, as well as graphs, charts, and statistics to illustrate conclusions. I'd appreciate receiving the revision by 2/1/94. Suggest you rename the report "Departmental Dividends."

*Scenario:* Ramona Finch has several memo pads. One is headed "R. Finch, CFO" for no-nonsense situations. When a cap pistol will suffice in lieu of a big gun, she uses less formal memo head.

To:      Hugh Sharif
From:    Ramona Finch

Forgive me for taking so long to thank you for your excellent and perceptive work in providing those union-related documents. We found them very helpful during the negotiations, especially Document D.

Please let me know if you happen to uncover any more revealing records concerning the union or other issues you feel I should know about.

Finch is masterful. She begins by asking for Hugh's pardon, which makes him feel important, and refers specifically to Document D, of which he is most proud. Her use of *we* suggests that others are aware of Hugh's "excellent and perceptive work." Finally, she sets him up as her personal spy.

A particularly impressive memo pad was the bible in which President Ronald Reagan inscribed a message (dated October 3, 1986) to the Iranians ending with ". . . all the nations shall be blessed in you."

# Borrowing Leverage

*I used not only all the brains I have, but all I can borrow.*

WOODROW WILSON

Calling cards, letterheads, and company logos are obvious attempts to borrow leverage: they establish our connection to something bigger and make our jobs a little easier. We also borrow leverage from supervisors on the corporate totem pole for the same reasons.

If you are not known to your target, you may be able to assume a mantle of power for yourself or borrow leverage from a generic threat, such as a lawyer.

> Sir—
>
> Your invoice is inappropriate. As a decision-making executive in a prominent corporation, I regularly encounter false and improper claims and have the resources to deal with them effectively.
>
> Any further attempts on your part to extract payment for a service which was not performed to my satisfaction will be met by my own claim for restitution, as well as letters to the Chamber of Commerce, the Better Business Bureau, and the local media.
>
> I would suggest that you agree to complete the job properly or write it off as a learning experience.
>
> —A. W. Fels

> Sir—
>
> Your persistent attempts to extract payment for a service which was not completed to my satisfaction are misguided and, according to my attorney, improper.
>
> Any future harassment of this nature will be turned over to my attorney for action.
>
> —Dr. A. Fels

A more effective form of borrowed leverage is to use a name that is meaningful to your target. At the office, this may be your target's boss, the CEO, or another of "those who must be obeyed."

*Scenario:* Don Flexor, the company controller, was entering the elevator as Hugh, an employee, was getting out. Hugh briefly mentioned an idea of his. Wanting to go to Boston next week, Hugh levers this brief meeting into a manipulative memo to his supervisor, Arnold.

> Arnold—
>
> Don Flexor and I were discussing the idea of my taking a close look at how quarterly closing procedures are handled at the Boston office. It probably won't take more than a day or two.
>
> Unless I hear differently, I'll plan on Thursday and Friday for this trip.
>
> —Hugh

If Arnold took the time to ask Flexor whether he talked to Hugh about going to Boston, Flexor would have to admit that the topic did come up.

Leverage can be applied to gain still more leverage. Suppose Hugh's motive was to remind Arnold that he has friends in high places. He might ask for nothing in return—this time.

> Arnold—
>
> Don Flexor and I were discussing the way quarterly closing procedures are handled at the Boston office. I suggested bringing you in on this and he agreed.
>   Can we get together to discuss it on Thursday?
> —Hugh

The source of leverage must be meaningful to the target. Archibald MacLeish observed this in 1957 when he and his literary friends, Ernest Hemingway among them, were trying to obtain a pardon for Ezra Pound from U.S. Attorney General Herbert Brownell.

> To:    Ernest Hemingway
> From:  Archibald MacLeish
> Dear Pappy,
>
> Enclosed is the letter I wrote you about. It seemed wise and now seems even wiser to have three signers only—you and [Robert] Frost and [T. S.] Eliot.
>   I don't know much about Brownell but I should guess he would be more apt to respond to the suggestion of three highly meaningful names than to a column of signatures.
> —Archie
>                                              Winnick, pp. 392–93

## Testimony

> *The louder he talked of his honor, the faster we counted the spoons.*
>
> RALPH WALDO EMERSON

Borrowing leverage from the owner of a large following is an attempt to gain some of that following by association. Politicians exploit this strategy when they decorate their public images with well-known entertainers.

When you see a person on TV wearing a white coat and recommending a drug, you're tempted to accept the "doctor's" views as expert opinion, ignoring the fact that an actor was selected for appearance, personality, and presentation skills and paid to promote the drug by the company that produced and sells it.

Testimony, although it may not carry a lot of weight, can add spice to memos. You may select from resources that are internal (annual, financial, or departmental reports) or external (scientific, industry-specific, or media references) to your organization.

> According to our *Personnel Guidelines*, we should meet within the next few days to discuss my evaluation.

> According to the *Annual Report*, our prime concern is quality.

> According to *Industry Annual*, the average starting salary in our business is . . .

> According to the CEO of Ford in *The Times*, the challenge of the international marketplace is . . .

## Attachments

> *Nothing in fine print is ever good news.*
>
> ANDY ROONEY

You can bolster your point by borrowing leverage from an attachment.

> A comparison of the latest computer printouts (stack attached) to the earlier reports (also attached) clearly suggests a cost overrun in excess of 10 percent.

> I find nothing in the relevant sections of *Robert's Rules of Order* (copy attached) to support your contention.

> There are a lot of small companies in and around Portland that might be interested in our services (Portland Yellow Pages attached).

An attachment is especially useful if it cites an earlier statement or position written by your target.

> Your long-range plan includes the mission statement that . . .

> In agreement with our corporate personnel policies (copy attached), my position on . . .

*Scenario:* Vicky wants to get a jump on her colleagues by gaining early access to the company's annual report. She'd also like to exercise some influence over its content. She sends a note to Hal, who approves the final report before it's produced.

> To:     Hal
> From:   Vicky
>
> My view on the importance of proper use of language in our *Annual Report* was echoed by William Safire in his recent "On Language" column (*New York Times Magazine* section).
>     William and I are in complete agreement that exaggerations such as "putting out 110% of effort" (see page 4, line 6 of last year's Annual Report) and "striving to achieve a higher level of perfection" (page 7, line 19) are inappropriate.
>     Clearly, the *Annual Report* should be edited by a member of the management team with strong language skills. For this reason, it has been suggested that the final copy pass across my desk before being sent on to the printer.

Vicky's name-dropping capitalizes on Safire's reputation and literary expertise by quoting him, albeit out of context. She weaves Safire's comments into a semblance of agreement with her own point of view, suggesting that she and William are on a first-name basis and that his agreement extends to their *Annual Report.*

Even if your attachment has no relevance to the matter at hand, the perception of its relevance may lend credibility to your argument by redirecting your target's attention.

*Scenario:* Don Flexor, the controller, receives a memo from Ramona Finch, the CFO, requesting a special end-of-fiscal-year audit. He's already running late on the revised year-to-date budget which the vice president of marketing has been waiting for impatiently. Recognizing an opportunity to get off the hook, the controller sends a memo to the vice president, N. E. Johansson, who is above him and below Finch on the organization chart.

> To:     N. E. Johansson, Vice President
> From:   Don Flexor, Controller
>
> Sorry about the slight delay of revised year-to-date budget figures. I'll supply them as soon as we've completed the special audit request—note attached memo.

Although the attached memo on the special end-of-fiscal-year audit had nothing to do with Flexor's delay in revising the YTD budget, the impression is created that the delay was caused by the CFO's directive.

Alternatively, Flexor decides to offer Johansson a trade: the budget Johansson wants for Johansson's support on an unrelated matter.

> To:     N. E. Johansson, Vice President
> From:   Don Flexor, Controller
>
> As you can see from Finch's memo (attached), I will be tied up for a while on other matters.
>     In order to give your YTD budget revision the attention it deserves, I'll need to fill my vacant deputy controller slot immediately, despite the hiring freeze.
>     Can I count on your support when I confront the board?

The controller sends this memo and attachment in an interoffice envelope that was last addressed to Finch. The interoffice envelope, routed from Finch to Flexor to Johansson, creates the impression that the contents were initiated by the powerful Ramona Finch. With this borrowed leverage, Flexor knows that Johansson will at least open the envelope.

## CC's

> *Expert advice is a great comfort, even when it's wrong.*
>
> ELLEN CURRIE

Although actual *carbon* copies are rarely seen these days, cc lists are still a mainstay of corporate communications. A cc may be used to inform the recipient of an action or be a powerful weapon with the subliminal message of "I feel I must cover myself in my dealings with you and gain someone else's support."

The composition and format of the cc list can be used to make a statement: you claim alliance with the people you select and their positions. The ordering of names can be revealing if not in alphabetical order or by organizational rank.

*Scenario:* Anatoly has been researching competitive strategies under the direction of his boss, Mr. Korsch. His goal is to get some data from Gary, who reports to Mr. Campo.

If Anatoly's goal is to get the information from a cooperative colleague and share the rewards with Gary, he would not send any cc's. However, Anatoly may want to use Gary's information to enhance his own reputation.

👎 To:     Gary
   From:   Anatoly

Your data is needed for the completion of the competitive
strategies report assigned to me by Mr. Korsch. In particular,
I will need your opening innovations by Friday, May 1.

This memo suggests that Anatoly intends to appropriate Gary's work for
his own ends. Anatoly could write a less hostile memo with a cc to his
boss to reassure Gary and give him credit for his work.

👍 To:     Gary
   cc:     Mr. Korsch
   From:   Anatoly

I need your opening innovations for the completion of the
competitive strategies report assigned to me by Mr. Korsch.
My deadline is Friday, May 1.

If Anatoly believes that the information will not be forthcoming from
Gary, he might cc Gary's boss, Mr. Campo. Anatoly is being up front by
sending his own boss a cc, thereby covering himself if there is any resentment from Gary because of Anatoly's pressure or from Mr. Campo
because of the inference.

This approach, however, delivers a negative message to both Gary and
Mr. Campo, suggesting that Anatoly feels that Gary needs to be pressured. Because Anatoly needs the data, he believes the cc is necessary to
shake Gary into action. Anatoly can cover himself by including a cc for
his own boss.

Used in a positive manner, carbon copies can be productive and well
received.

👍 To:     Gary
   cc:     Mr. Campo, Mr. Korsch
   From:   Anatoly

Thank you for sharing your opening innovations data for the
competitive strategies report.
     Your material was concise and well-presented, and forms the bulk
of Part 2. You are given credit in the text.

A possible twist to this scenario might occur if Gary supplied poorly
conceived materials to Anatoly. Anatoly might distance himself from
Gary's work with a humble acknowledgment.

👍 To:      Gary
cc:      Mr. Campo, Mr. Korsch
From:    Anatoly

Thank you for sharing your opening innovations data for the
competitive strategies report.
    As this is your material, I did not integrate it, but recommended
it to readers of the competitive strategies report.

An extremely manipulative use of the cc is the sleight-of-hand technique in which the cc is sent and the letter is not. We have heard of a
manager who wanted to impress his boss with his toughness but also
wanted to avoid upsetting his staff. This person wrote a strongly worded
memo to the staff with a cc to the boss—without ever sending the original to the staff. Thus, he made himself known to upper management as a
"tough" executive while remaining a "nice guy" to his staff.

A blind cc (bcc) is usually meant to inform the recipient of your
actions. For example, you may want to routinely bcc a new boss until you
have established mutual trust. But blind cc's can have disastrous results if
knowledge of them passes beyond the sender and receiver.

In the previous scenario, Anatoly might have decided to send a bcc to
Bobby, a prominent member of the policy committee who will be reviewing his report. When Gary forwarded the information to Anatoly, he
might have sent a bcc to another member of the policy committee. If the
two recipients compared notes, however, they would resent being manip-
ulated and it is not likely that they'd quickly forget.

If you list your cc's, you avoid a potential battle.

*Scenario:* When Warner swallowed Time, the new chairman learned that
some traditions had to be digested slowly.

To:      Dick Munro [ Time Warner Chairman]
cc:      Time Inc. Board
From:    Andrew Heiskell [Time Chairman]
Date:    11/9/87

You came into my office to tell me you were remodeling the 34th
floor reception room and that the Donovan and Heiskell portraits
were to be taken down. Furthermore, you said there would be no
other place in Time Inc. where they could hang. You added that
Henry Luce's picture would also go. I believe you said something
like "this is a different world, you know."

Indeed it is, and what management does with today's Time Inc. is obviously its responsibility.

However, Time Inc.'s history belongs to the corporation, not its current management. And rewriting history is not part of our company tradition.

I hope and trust you can find a way of accommodating these elements of Time Inc. history and heritage. Clurman, p. 24

Munro called to apologize before Heiskell had a chance to send the copies to the board members.

# 6

# Camouflage

*Men should not know how their laws or sausages are made.*

OTTO VON BISMARK

Camouflage is nature's way of dressing a potential lunch as something not to eat, and of attracting a potential victim. In the business environment, we wear camouflage to protect a weakness or to emphasize a strength. The way we represent ourselves and the manner in which we deal with others help us blend into—or stand out from—our surroundings.

There is no perfect camouflage for every situation. The perfectly concealed predator would starve if it failed to attract a tasty victim. Similarly, while a low-profile personal style may protect you from attack, it may also leave you starved for recognition and reward.

Appearance, attitude, and humor can be employed as camouflage. Use them to encourage others to cooperate with you and to discourage any inclinations they may have to make your life more difficult.

## Appearance

*When you get right down to it, excellent performance on the job is not usually the basic consideration in advancement. Instead, it's the impression of excellence that you create with your superiors.*

RICHARD LATHROP

Your appearance—the way you look, your behavior and mannerisms—affect other people's perceptions of you and your accomplishments.

Appearance can and often does outweigh reality, as people may evaluate you and judge your work by external flags rather than actual achievement. Physical characteristics aside, you can assure that your personal style and the image you project contribute positively to your appearance.

## Style

> *The notes I handle no better than many pianists. But the pauses between the notes—ah, that is where the art resides!*
>
> ARTHUR SCHNABEL

The Texas businessman who adapts his pitch to Japanese custom scores more points in Yokohama than the businessman with a folksy drawl; a wealthy political candidate gets more mileage in a Chicago tavern by chugging ale than by sipping Courvoisier. People react to your personal style of responding. You may appear abrupt and brash, talkative, or quiet. Your style might even be a combination of these, depending on the circumstances of your choosing.

The bull has a tendency to be abrupt. Although his intention is to get the job done as efficiently as possible, his style is often taken as rudeness and insensitivity by his staff and colleagues.

To:     Staff
From:   Bill

Get it done by 9 A.M. Friday.

The bull could modify his tone without appearing indecisive.

To:     Staff
From:   Bill

I would appreciate your getting it done by 9 A.M. Friday so I can meet our regional deadline.

The magpie tends to ramble on without a clearly defined objective.

To:     Tom, Dick, Harry, and Eustice
From:   Maggie

There are a number of issues that need to be clarified. I'll have to meet with each of you individually to cover all the points, and then we can all meet together to decide when it may be feasible to get it done.

The staff would have a better idea of what was expected of them if magpie could be more specific.

👍 To:      Tom, Dick, Harry, and Eustice
From:   Maggie

The following issues need to be clarified:
      Tom:  production costs
      Dick:  deadlines
      Harry:  sales projections
      Eustice:  QA
I'll set up a schedule to meet with each of you next week, and then for all of us to meet together to draft a final agenda.

The clam seeks to avoid conflict, even at the risk of failing to get the job done.

👎 To:      Maggie
From:   Clem

You know how much I liked the plan you prepared last month. There are a few problems with this one, Maggie, but I'm sure they can be easily resolved. I've noted the corrections and changes I would like you to make. Can you give me the corrected version by Friday afternoon? Please feel free to call on me if you need any additional help.

The clam needs to recognize that the earlier and more firmly a potential problem is addressed, the less of a problem it is apt to become, and that identifying a problem isn't necessarily confrontational.

👍 To:      Maggie
From:   Clem

This month's plan falls short of the one you prepared last month in that the sales projections were incomplete and the text was not thoroughly edited. I have noted the corrections and changes to be made. Please give me the corrected version by Friday afternoon, and feel free to call on me if you have any questions.

The chameleon alters and mixes styles depending on the circumstances. It's hard to know where you stand with someone who changes stripes in full stride.

To:      Clem
From:   Chameleon

The plan is unacceptable. You'll have to clean it up and return it to me by 9 A.M. Friday. Clem, you know how much I liked the last plan you prepared, the one on financial projections. It was well researched and presented. Well, I've noted some of the corrections and changes to be made to this one, but I don't have the time to rewrite it myself. Let me know if you anticipate any problems getting this done on time, or if you would prefer to be relieved of the responsibility altogether.

Flexibility does not mean inconsistency. The chameleon will get better results with a more evenhanded approach.

 To:      Clem
From:   Chameleon

The plan needs to be rewritten according to the corrections and changes I have indicated. Also, I am counting on you to identify and fix any other inconsistencies along these same lines. Please let me know as soon as possible if you anticipate any problems getting this done by 9 A.M. Friday.

## Image

> *To be champ, you have to believe in yourself when nobody else will.*
>
> SUGAR RAY ROBINSON

Although you may consider yourself to be a competent person, it is the *image* of competence that will carry you much further than your actual skill level.

Written documents, especially your memos, make a lasting contribution to your image of being a competent, confident colleague. A memo that is not clear in purpose will not promote an image of confidence.

*Scenario:* Cecily expresses more frustration than useful information in a request to her boss, Mike.

 To:      Mike
From:   Cecily
Re:      New Office Equipment

I was determined to get a few words on paper concerning the need for some new equipment in the office. I have come to the conclusion that we need quite a bit, and so I am attaching a list and my thoughts on the necessity for each.

Fortunately, Cecily took the time to rewrite her recommendations in a more objective manner. The revised version certainly makes Cecily appear more competent and professional.

To:    Mike
From:  Cecily
Re:    New Office Equipment

Attached is a list of what we need and a rationale.

Total cost of equipment: $23,596.

*Scenario:* Ben uses numbered lists to present his information in a logical structure to appear competent.

To:    Staff
From:  Ben
Re:    R. P. Inc.'s firing of their president, F. J.

You have individually asked me about the firing of the president of our major competitor. There appear to have been three basic reasons for what happened:

1. As chairman of the board and principal stockholder, R. P. has serious problems with the management philosophy of the new administration.
2. Under F. J., profitability decreased from 11.2 % in 1990 to 6.5% this year.
3. F. J. divorced R. P.'s daughter.

*Scenario:* Dierdre is a competent and reliable manager in the Purchasing department. Frustrated in her ability to reach her career goals, she sets out to enhance her corporate image. Dierdre's professional interest is cost control, and she is also a talented computer systems analyst. She targets the CEO, Mr. Terseman, and develops a brief profile of him through observation and discrete questioning of her colleagues. He is reputed to have a strong preference for concise presentations, and to make quick decisions when so inclined.

Dierdre does her homework to develop a cost-saving plan that extends beyond her own department. She draws on her professional background, borrows from some friends in data processing, and comes up with a no-nonsense proposal. The material is submitted to the CEO in a bright yellow binder (the color of her target's favorite tie) and summarized in a succinctly worded memo.

> To:      Jeffrey Terseman, CEO
> cc:       Head Purchasing
> From:   Dierdre Durite, Purchasing Department
> Re:       Business Simulation Algorithm
>
> Attached is my proposal for a computer system algorithm for cost control across all departments in our company.
>
> Cost of implementation: $53,569
>
> Savings in first year: $124,568
>
> Savings in 3–5 subsequent years: $225,000
>
> The basis of this proposal has been evaluated and approved by staff members of the IBM Research and Development Facility in Yorktown Heights.
>
> I will call your office Tuesday morning to arrange a meeting on this proposal.
>
> Attachments:
>> IBM R&D Review
>> Goal Overview
>> Proposal Detail
>> Capital investment schedule
>> Cash flow analysis
>> Development history

Conveying the image of a competent, well-organized professional can help you get more of what you want.

# Attitude

*Don't be so humble, you're not that great.*

GOLDA MEIR

The way you think, feel, and act toward others is expressed by your gestures and words in conversation, and in your written communications. Although you cannot force people to like you, you can at least be considerate of those around you. The basic formula is to appear courteous, interested, and sensitive to their needs and aspirations.

A simple "please" or "thank you" is the weave that binds the social fabric together in both oral and written communication. These considerations are expected in a business environment, and their absence is boorish.

👎 Can you process this request . . .

👍 Can you please process this request . . .

👎 I received your reference on . . .

👍 Thanks for your help on . . .

Consideration also means acknowledging others and allowing them their own goals and pursuits. Infringing invites resentment and retaliation.

👎 Lila—

I received your memo about coming to the forthcoming committee meeting. Aren't you more involved with human resources? Well, this meeting addresses only technical matters.

I'll send you a copy of the minutes which will tell you when the policy and funding session is scheduled.

—Pete

Rather than appearing to block Lila from attending the meeting, Pete could instead offer her the benefit of his knowledge and resources.

👍 Lila—

I appreciate your willingness to participate in the forthcoming committee meeting, but were you aware that this meeting addresses only technical matters? (See attached agenda.)

Since I recall your having expressed an interest in personnel issues, particularly policy and funding, I'm also attaching a copy of the agenda for the next human resources meeting.

I'll send you a copy of the minutes of the technical meeting if any policy and funding issues are discussed.

—Pete

Most people like to feel needed and are quick to help when you ask for their assistance or advice—especially if you pay attention to the advice when it is offered.

Mario—

Since you have always been a strong supporter of women's rights,

I want to ask your opinion on a delicate and confidential issue. As a friend and long-time supporter, I assure you that your response will be kept in the strictest of confidence.

What would be your feelings about the establishment of a Feminist Party as an alternative to the D's and R's? I'm only looking for your immediate reaction, not a commitment at this time.

—Alesia

Showing interest in other people is likely to earn you support while defusing potential trouble. Though you cannot develop a deep feeling for everyone in the office, it is possible to keep up with the private concerns of a few selected individuals. A birthday card, friendly inquiry, or offer of help can work wonders for your relationships with your coworkers.

*Scenario:* Pandora is a sales rep in the Midwest working for the regional manager, Luis. She would like to return to the Boston area, where she grew up, and learns that the Boston territory may be opening. The personnel manager has mentioned that one of the big problems with all the urban territories is that a nonnative has major problems with geography. Pandora sends Luis a memo complaining about her territory being so large she hardly has any time left for herself. The boss responds.

Pandora—

Yes, I know how large Ohio and Indiana are, which makes your recent performance all the more impressive. Frankly, I am proud of the way you stepped in and took charge of your accounts, and I'm going to do my best to see that your efforts are recognized by the company.

—Luis

The operative word is *proud.* With this memo, Luis solves one problem with stroking. Pandora now feels free to stroke in return—she isn't about to throw in the towel and she converts his own words to her advantage.

Luis—

Thank you for your encouragement. Ever since I joined the company, I have always felt you were looking out for me. That's why I can only hope that you will find a way to help me transfer closer to the Boston area as soon as possible.

There will be two major benefits to this move:

1. Coming from that part of the country, I know my way around.

2. Being near the home office would give me a better opportunity
   to pick up your sales techniques.
—Pan

Even when you know you're being handed a line, it's still difficult to resist the ploy of being admired and relied upon.

# Humor

*Laughter is a tranquilizer with no side effects.*

ARNOLD H. GLASOW

In the movie *Good Morning, Vietnam*, an officer who is excused from his temporary role of disk jockey protests, "In my heart I know I'm funny." If you believe you're Mirth Incorporated, we advise you to find out if you appear funny to others.

Light humor and other verbal bantering can help you fit in with your colleagues, distract attention, smooth a path through bad times, and help you get on with your job. But it is a two-edged sword with potentially disastrous effects when carried to extremes.

Written humor is especially susceptible to misinterpretation. It tends to work better between people who know each another than among strangers because you can anticipate the response and determine if it is likely to further your objective. Is your target amenable to humor? Is he apt to get the joke? Is her sense of humor compatible with yours?

👎 Dear Ms. Jennetti—
   First the garbage men walked out. Then your request for additional information arrived.

👍 Harvey—
   Remember the ball game that was rained out and we had to wait weeks for the rescheduled game? For some reason, your request for additional information reminded me of it.

Humor can cover incompetence or delays by derailing your target's attention from an issue you don't want to—or can't—respond to directly.

👎 Pat—
   I'll get your figures as soon as I can.

Pat—

> This year is unbelievable . . . we've packed more widgets than I have hairs on my head.
>     I'll get your figures as soon as I can.

Humor can eliminate resistance and allow you to proceed with your point of view.

*Scenario:* One of the things that really bothers John is that Gregg lacks a sense of humor when he gets onto one of his "environmental conscience" rides.

 To:      John
From:   Gregg
Re:       Proposed Manufacturing Process

> The environmental damage of this process will haunt our company and the Earth for years to come.

 To:      John
From:   Gregg
Re:       Cloning the Earth

> I am attaching an article by Buck Artwald on "Cloning the Earth." I think that this is a viable concept that our company should endorse, especially if we go ahead with the proposed new manufacturing process.
>     Let's look at the benefits of this article.

Double entendres dealing with sex, politics, and religion tend to be offensive and have negative results.

 Lila—

> Congratulations on the promotion—what did it cost you? (only kidding)

An urge to add a parenthetical apology should be warning enough to avoid the "joke."

Belittling someone else's achievement will earn you more hostility and retribution than respect and cooperation.

 Lila—

> Congratulations on the promotion, if you can call being east of the Rockies a promotion.

Inoffensive humor is more apt to raise a smile.

 Lila—

> Congratulations on your promotion. I'm sure you will enjoy your
> new locale.
> Too bad the mountains in Aspen will block your view.

We often depend on clichés to make our thoughts known, but their overfamiliarity make them easy to dismiss—along with the intended point. Clichés can be twisted slightly to alter or reverse their meaning and draw your reader's attention back to where you want it, as in Tom Weller's "Two heads are more numerous than one" and the anonymous "Gentlemen prefer blondes to balds." Your meaning must be clear, and it should be obvious to the reader that the twist was intentional or the message will be abandoned.

> A king's castle is his home.

> It's better to have loved and won.

Sarcasm is caustic, although less risky, when the recipient has no power over the writer. You might be sarcastic with a subscription service that continually scrambles your billings, but you are not likely to chance your future on a sarcastic quip to your boss.

Bennett Cerf and Alexander Woollcott were close friends with a history of jousting humor.

> Dear Cerf:
>
> By some miracle you have published a book which is not second
> rate. Please send me twelve copies at once.
> Yours sincerely,
>
> A. Woollcott

Cerf responded:

> Dear Woollcott:
>
> By some miracle you can buy those twelve copies at Brentano's.
> Yours very truly,
>
> Bennett Cerf

Tepper, p. 5

# Fitting In and Standing Out

*You have to work things out in the cloakroom and when you've got them worked out you can debate a little before you vote.*

SENATE MAJORITY LEADER LYNDON JOHNSON

Generally, it is an advantage to blend into your milieu, as long as you don't drift into obscurity. When can camouflage be safely set aside? Only when the potential payoff is high enough to justify the risk.

*Scenario:* Pfeiffer is an account representative who has been on leave for nearly a month. In Pfeiffer's absence, a large account was lost. Seltzer, another account rep, was asked by the boss, Goodbody, to step in and try to repair the damage. Seltzer has managed to win back the account, and Goodbody sends him a congratulatory memo.

> To:     Abner Seltzer
> From:   P. Goodbody
> Nice work, Abner. It's a good thing we had you around!

If Seltzer wanted to promote his career as an account rep, he might draft a memo that exhibits confidence while he plants himself firmly in the driver's seat. Seltzer recognizes that he can scuttle or exonerate Pfeiffer, maybe even negotiate a raise. He can also draw fire from jealous colleagues or conservative superiors if he isn't careful.

> To:     Ms. Goodbody
> From:   Mr. Seltzer
> The new advertising director and I seem to get along pretty well,
> and I recommend that my appointment be made permanent ASAP.

A memo like this, while clear and to the point, might appear abrupt to Ms. Goodbody, and would definitely appear as a power grab to any supporters of Pfeiffer.

> To:     Ms. Goodbody
> From:   Mr. Seltzer
> Thank you for your kind words. I was only doing my job, but it is
> gratifying when one's efforts are rewarded.

> The new advertising director and I seem to get along pretty well;
> he invited me to play golf with him next week.

This pleasant acknowledgment of praise minimizes Seltzer's interest in Pfeiffer's position, while it leaves him free to present a case for his permanent appointment at a later time.

After some reflection, Seltzer realizes that he doesn't want a career as an account rep but would rather pursue a career in advertising. Given this goal, Seltzer could simply dismiss his accomplishment by suggesting that it could have been done by anyone.

 To:      Ms. Goodbody
From:   Mr. Seltzer

> It was no big deal—I was only standing in for Pfeiffer who could
> probably done it if he hadn't been on paternity leave.

This memo would alienate him from the department, and its patronizing tone could draw a personal attack from Pfeiffer or even Goodbody.

Rather than waste an opportunity, Seltzer lays the groundwork to enlist Ms. Goodbody in his career change.

 To:      Ms. Goodbody
From:   Mr. Seltzer

> Despite the fact that I am most interested in advertising, I have
> been fascinated by the work of your account reps and I thoroughly
> enjoyed filling in for Pfeiffer during his leave. In terms of the
> account, I simply did what I thought you yourself would have done
> in a like situation.
>      Thank you for your kind words—it's always gratifying when one's
> efforts are recognized by someone with your level of experience.

Later, Seltzer follows up to ask Ms. Goodbody's help.

 Ms. Goodbody—

> Now that Pfeiffer is coming back, I'd like to sit down with you and
> get your advice on my transfer to advertising.
>      Could we get together tomorrow afternoon?
> —Seltzer

# 7

# Bayonets and Boomerangs

*Today's colleague may be tomorrow's boss.*
ARNOLD PAPADOUPOULOS

Successful and unsuccessful people have occasion to use specialized tools. The former know how and when to employ these tools to their advantage. Apologies, rumors, offers to help, refusals, and threats may easily backfire if not used with special care.

## Making Apologies

*Aim for the eagle, bag the pheasant, and never eat crow.*
OLIVER REDTAIL

Apologies may be necessary when a person or a group has not performed as expected: forgetting a commitment, missing a delivery date, or failing to produce a report on schedule. Typically, there is mutual acknowledgment of the deficiency, with anger or frustration on one side and guilt on the other.

It is essential to relieve these tensions. When possible, this is best done face-to-face, a courtesy that is effective and leaves no permanent record. Sometimes, however, apologies must be offered in writing. At such times, check to make sure the message appears sincere and will satisfy the recipient. The first of the following examples smacks of a lie; the second falls short of satisfying; the third accepts responsibility without blame or apology.

👎 The check is in the mail.

I am sorry I didn't mail your check.

 We regret that your check was lost in the mail. This should not have happened.

Any apology tacitly accepts blame, but an apology that accepts responsibility bravely appears noble without accepting fault. Janet Reno, the Secretary of the Justice Department, received superb press by accepting responsibility for the Waco, Texas disaster, and Harry Truman's "the buck stops here" is a classic example of accepting responsibility while effectively precluding blame (except by some Republicans).

*Scenario:* An unfortunate note was sent to the entire staff by a receptionist and must be redressed.

> To:     Staff
> From:  Reception/Switchboard
>
> The function of the switchboard has been taken for granted. Therefore I am forced to do the following:
>
>    I will no longer leave the board in search of visitors.
>
>    I will no longer search for a staff member.
>
>    I will no longer hold messages at my desk.
>
>    I WILL NOT TAKE MESSAGES.

Compare how two different managers might handle this blast from the receptionist who reports to the office manager.

> To:     Staff
> From:  W. Bullhead, Office Manager
>
> I'm really sorry about the memo you received recently about the handling of phone messages. Of course the switchboard will take messages. I regret the confusion. It would help, however, if you would let the board know about your comings and goings.

Bullhead deserts the operator and fails to resolve the problem. Even more critically, he fails to engender team spirit by requesting only the staff's compliance.

By contrast, the following response is supportive of the operator (indeed, the position *had* been taken for granted) and creates a team feeling to support the switchboard. D. D. Wright recognizes a problem and proposes a solution to benefit all concerned.

To:     Staff
From:   D. D. Wright, Office Administration

Paula reacted by trying to shock us into an awareness of the problems she is facing at the switchboard. She will, by the way, take messages if necessary, but please do keep her informed of your absences.

*Scenario:* Thomas Paine was a harsh critic of President George Washington's politics. In 1796, when Paine believed that the American leader had deceived him and others, Paine offered no apologies for this scathing memo.

From:   Thomas Paine
To:     George Washington

As censure is but awkwardly softened by apology, I shall offer you no apology for this letter. The eventful crisis to which your double politics have conducted the affairs of your country, requires an investigation untrammeled by ceremony.                    Schuster, p. 43

# Spreading Rumors

*Nothing is so firmly believed as that which is least known.*

FRANCIS JEFFREY

The use of rumor is an insidious weapon, but it is a double-edged sword: it can devastate its target, and the ramifications can boomerang right back at you. A reputation as a rumormonger will diminish your credibility even as you try to tarnish the credibility of your target.

Still, rumors can work advantageously in some situations. A question hinting at the activities of a rival may just help you to open some closed doors in your company. Often the threat of competition will provoke a very positive response.

Did you hear that Zort Company is starting a new multi-level marketing operation?

When you decide to use the grapevine for your own ends, find a way to plant your information without being identified as the source. A rumor on marketing will have little credence if attributed to a person known to be pushing for marketing innovation.

To publicize your rumor, you can plant it in a public location, such as near the photocopier or water cooler. If your target has the habit of poking through your office, you can plant a memo to yourself, a draft to someone else, or one from someone else to you. Positioned on your desk or made visible within an open drawer, your misinformation will have added credibility because it appears to have been unearthed without your knowledge. You can hardly be confronted about the validity of such materials.

*Scenario:* Burt wants to encourage Arnold to purchase new computers, but knows that Arnold would be suspicious of a direct request. Instead, Burt plants a memo on the corner of his desk, knowing Arnold has roving eyes when he passes by Burt's desk.

> Felicia—
> How can we get Arnold to order those new computers? We all agree that they could help us produce the best results this department ever had, making him (and all the rest of us) look good. The problem is he always suspects me of ulterior motives. He never realizes how much I try to help him.
> —Burt

*Scenario:* Felicia borrows leverage from Flexor, the controller, to suggest that her voice is heard on high. She leaves a handwritten note on her desk, where her supervisor Arnold is certain to spot it.

> Ask Flexor to include Arnold in the meeting.

Positive illusions can be created by responding to memos that exist only in your fantasies.

*Scenario:* Arnold's boss has been transferred to Cincinnati, and everyone is speculating on his replacement. Hugh sees this as an opportunity to raise his status with Arnold, his supervisor, who is known to check out the desks of his group most evenings. Hugh scribbles the following memo, with corrections, to appear as a draft.

> To:     Ramona Finch, CFO
> From:   Hugh Sharif
> Thank you for your support. I do not want to appear ungrateful, but this does not appear to be the right opportunity for me at this time.

> Aside from causing strained feelings with some of my long-time colleagues, I might be better off scaling the ladder one rung at a time.

Once he is sure Arnold has seen the memo—which is obvious from Arnold's increased deference toward Hugh—Hugh takes it home to include in his memoirs.

Rumors can sink reputations and wash careers aground. Because rumor requires no substantiation, defending against it is nearly impossible. Should you be on the receiving end of a personal rumor, your best efforts may lead to further spreading of the misinformation. The only way to discredit a rumor is by debunking it in detail.

*Scenario:* Jane has heard a rumor that she received her recent promotion because of an alleged relationship with her boss. She sends her boss a memo:

> Bill—
>
> I've recently heard a rumor that my promotion is a result of intimacy with you.
>
> To reaffirm the basis of this promotion, would you please review the attached promotion announcement. If it is acceptable to you, I would appreciate your signing and distributing it widely.
> —Jane
> Attachment [a convincing summary of her qualifications and experience for the job]

By posting this announcement, Jane is emphasizing her qualifications. People will be inclined to accept her promotion and to dismiss the rumor.

Jane believes that the receptionist may be responsible for spreading, if not originating, the rumor. She has no evidence with which to confront the woman, so she composes a manipulative memo.

> Paula—
>
> As fantastic as this may sound, there seems to be a nasty rumor going around about me and another member of the staff. This sort of thing doesn't do anyone in the company any credit and it's a disservice to the few women who have earned responsible positions like yours and mine.
>
> Since you see everyone during the course of the day, can I count on you to help put a stop to this if anyone should bring it up?
>
> Thanks for whatever help you're able to give.
> —Jane

# Offering Help

*The most difficult thing in the world is to know how to
do a thing and to watch someone else doing it wrong
without comment.*

THEODORE H. WHITE

If you recognize a personal shortcoming and want to correct it, you may
decide to ask for guidance.  If you don't recognize the shortcoming and
others offer to help, you are likely to call the advice unwarranted and
consider the offerer a busybody.  There is a tendency to reject both
unwanted advice and the person providing it.

People long entrenched in their positions may have a paternal urge to
offer advice to newer members of the staff.

*Scenario:*  Bullhead has been the company's factotum since the time carbon paper was purchased in bulk.  As the company grew, his sense of
responsibility and paternalism has mushroomed.

To:      Hugh
From:   W. Bullhead

As the Office Manager, I want to welcome you to the company and
make myself available should you need anything in your transition.
    I am also attaching a little brochure that I have made up for new
employees, called *Office Management: The Font of All Necessities*.
I am sure that you will find this guide useful in guiding you through
our systems.
    Again, please call upon me for help.

This pompous memo is not likely to motivate a request for help.

Bullhead tries again with a memo that sounds sincere.  This offer of
assistance is more likely to be well received by the new employee.  From
Bullhead's perspective, his offer extends his own indispensability to the
company.

To:      Hugh
From:   W. Bullhead

Welcome to the company! As the office manager, I am available
should you need anything.
    Attached is a little guide to our systems that may be useful.
    Please call on me if I can be of any help.

This is about as far as Bullhead can reasonably go. He welcomes the new employee, provides a guide that might answer some questions, and offers to be available when needed.

Should a colleague ask for advice, avoid pressing your advice beyond the moment of receptivity.

 As you requested, I have marked up your report. Two questions that I had are noted on page 3.
I'd like to discuss this further and propose that we meet tomorrow after work so that I can elaborate on the changes needed.

The attempt to establish a specific time to follow up may not suit your colleague, and the offer to elaborate on recommendations appears too much like negative feedback. It would be better to leave the scheduling of the meeting to the person whose work you have been asked to evaluate, and to simply express sincere interest.

As you requested, I have marked up your report. Two questions that I had are noted on page 3.
I'd be glad to discuss this further if it's convenient for you.

After a series of such consultations, you might develop this association into an advantageous mentoring relationship—if you know where to draw the line in your offers of advice.

# Refusing

*In matters of principle, stand like a rock; in matters of taste, swim with the current.*

THOMAS JEFFERSON

Few organizations will accept an employee's blunt refusal to perform a task. If you must refuse, provide an escape hatch for the other person so that you are not seen as part of the problem. If you receive a refusal, you have to either ignore it or work around it.

*Scenario:* George in Product Development asks Nelson in Marketing for approval to test market a new chewing gum. Nelson has heard that the gum may have an abrasive effect on dentures and believes that George is not above using him as a scapegoat. He certainly does not want to endorse a product that could lead to questions of safety.

To:    George
From:  Nelson

There is no way that I can endorse a product for test-marketing that might have a problem in product safety.

Nelson in Marketing has no real way of evaluating product safety and this abrupt refusal does little more than establish him and his department as a bottleneck.

Rather than bluntly refusing, Nelson turns the problem of safety back to George and Product Development.

 To:    George
From:  Nelson

There is no way that I can evaluate the research results—I am not trained in this, while you are.
I look forward to test-marketing the gum, providing that you can ensure a clean bill of health regarding product safety.

*Scenario:* To avoid outright refusal, Bullhead uses procedures as an escape route. He sounds polite but insists on adherence to standard operating procedures.

To:    Hugh
From:  W. Bullhead

Your E-mail request for supplies is filled from our Gilboy warehouse based upon Supply Requisition Form 120C in triplicate.
I know that this is a nuisance, but please resubmit your request on that form.

The appearance of misunderstanding can sometimes be used in place of blatant refusal.

*Scenario:* Noel sees Chris, a new employee, in the company cafeteria. Chris is not interested in Noel's advances and tries to put Noel off in a friendly way. Waiting in Chris's mailbox is the following memo.

Chris—

Since you are new to the company, I would like to help you get acquainted with some people who would be good for you to know.
What time do you leave work?

—Noel

Noel seems pleasant enough, but Chris is not about to start socializing after office hours, knowing what that might lead to. On the other hand, Chris doesn't want to create an enemy with hurt feelings and so responds by ignoring the implied invitation (after work) and redirecting the focus.

> Noel—
>
> Thank you for your offer.
>     I'm sharing an office with Terry who was just hired and would also like to get to know some people in the other departments. Could we all get together for lunch next week?
>     We usually go at 12:15. Is that convenient for you?
>
> —Chris

Instead of outright refusal, you can use advice to serve as a diversion, as Abraham Lincoln did with his stepbrother.

> To:      John D. Johnson
> From:    Abraham Lincoln
>
> Your request for eighty dollars, I do not think it best to comply with now. . . . You are not lazy, and still you are an idler. I doubt whether since I saw you, you have done a good whole day's work, in any one day.
>     You have always been kind to me, and I do not now mean to be unkind to you. On the contrary, if you will but follow my advice, you will find it worth more than eight times eighty dollars to you.
>
> Schuster, pp. 311–12

# Threatening

*If you don't like the fire, don't light the match.*

WILLIAM (BILL) BULLHEAD

Blatant threats occasionally surface within the corporate circuit, and implied ones are a fact of everyday business life. Faced with this reality, a clever MMer should be able to counter a threat and avoid any negative repercussions.

No one can make threats with total impunity. Threats are resented, and eventually may be turned against you, no matter how powerful you are.

To:     Hugh
From:  W. Bullhead

Your continued E-mail requests are completely unacceptable and could result in your termination.

Bullhead's memo is counterproductive. His threat is questionable, in that he may not have the power to carry it through, and it is so blatant that anyone seeing it would side with Hugh.

To:     Hugh
From:  W. Bullhead

Your continued E-mail requests accomplish two things: they point up the problems with the system and they are not effective in getting your goals accomplished.
    Could you please use the forms?

Bullhead's second memo is not a threat, but rather a tersely polite refusal that offers Hugh a face-saving way out of the situation.
    For a threat to work, it must be directed at a target who has the power to comply—and who is willing to act.

To:     Bossman
From:  Joe

I have been talking with the Zort Company and have been offered a job at $40,000. I would like to stay here, but really must consider the economic impact on my family.
    As I am currently making $36,000, I am sure that you will be able to keep me with a 10 percent increase in my next paycheck.

Joe's bluff will probably be called before the next pay period. He may be of great value to the company, but the majority of supervisors will not respond well to this type of blackmail. Moreover, concurrence with this threat may be against a company policy unless Bossman *wants* to work around it.
    Joe could be more subtle in his approach.

To:     Bossman
From:  Joe

The Zort Company is looking for people with experience in a job description similar to ours. They are offering $40,000.
    According to our compensation schedule, a level 22 has a low of $23,000; a mid of $31,000; and a high of $39,000.

> Can we use the Zort example as justification to reevaluate our ranges?

This memo also carries an implied threat, but stops short of blackmail.

To be effective, the threat must be understood and considered as a possibility by the target. Joe's threat can be understood by Bossman, and the chances of his leaving are clearly real. Rasputin's warning memo was most likely ignored because he was not thought to be a credible threat.

> From:   Grigory Yefimovich Rasputin
> Date:   December 1916
>
> I feel that I shall leave life before January 1. . . . If I am murdered by nobles, for twenty-five years they will not wash their hands from my blood. Brothers will kill brothers . . . and for twenty-five years there will be no nobles in the country.                    Wilson, p. 189

Before the deadline, Rasputin was poisoned, then shot in the back and left for dead. He was shot twice again, kicked in the head as he attempted to fight back, beaten with a steel rod, and dumped through a hole in the ice—where he almost managed to untie his hands. He was then buried, exhumed, and burned.

For the record, he *was* murdered by nobles before January 1, and the Russian Revolution followed. Brothers did kill brothers and there have been no nobles in the country since.

Re: **Defense**

*Good defense always beats good offense.*

*Vince Lombardi*

An attack may be directed against our selves or our positions. An effective defense to either type of intrusion requires careful analysis, planning, and response; at times it may be better to preempt attacks than defend against them. Whatever you choose, manipulative memos can help you prevail.

# 8

# Defending Yourself

*Self defense is Nature's eldest law.*

JOHN DRYDEN

Researchers confirm that a large number of adults feel defenseless against a personal attack. This is true regardless of the validity of the attack.

Back in school, you surely noticed that some of the kids were always being picked on, while others never got flack from anyone. The difference between them was, of course, respect, whether for their accomplishments, their physical strength, or their personalities. Even if you couldn't identify the reason, you (and everybody else) just knew that a certain kid simply wasn't to be toyed with. Though the office scene is more subtle than the classroom, respect is still essential for well-being, and it comes to those who stand up for themselves.

## Responding to Unwarranted Attacks

*I would rather men should ask why no statue has been erected in my honor, than why one has.*

MARCUS CATO

Your attacker may be a habitual offender whose irritating manner is known to everyone who shares the office complex. But recall of verbal encounters is short and oral history is revisionist, so a written account will most likely stand as truth. Much as you may be tempted to trash an assailant's unjustified memo without responding, your attacker will have the last word unless you answer in writing.

To decide how to respond to an unwarranted attack, determine the intent. It's possible the attack is inspired by a perception of your vulnerability, motivated by malice, driven by insecurity, or based on misguided or erroneous information.

Then consider your position relative to that of your antagonist and the company itself. Your options extend from maintaining your dignity and composure to bending the protocols of courtesy and dealing with the attack in kind.

*Scenario:* Smythe receives an antagonistic note from Bundy, infested with insulting innuendos.

> Mr. Smythe—
>
> I am writing to advise you about the infamous computer project you're supposed to be in charge of.
>
> If you cared enough about this project, and the dedicated people who are giving their honest efforts to make it succeed, you would have begun paying attention to our valid suggestions. Who knows—you might even be able to salvage some small part of it.
>
> —Alex W. Bundy

Smythe cannot allow such impertinence to stand unanswered.

> Bundy—
>
> 1. There are indeed a number of dedicated people attached to the computer project.
> 2. I always follow up on suggestions with the individuals who make them.
> 3. Kindly concentrate on your job and leave mine to me.
>
> —R. S.

If Bundy had perceived Smythe to be vulnerable, he may now think otherwise.

Bundy's next memo has overtones of hostility, but it stops short of malice.

> Mr. Smythe—
>
> I understand that one of the key people on your team is transferring to another division. Perhaps we should discuss your staff problems before there are any more defections.
>
> —Alex W. Bundy

Smythe's tempered answer sets the record straight while offering a modicum of hope for Bundy in the future.

> Mr. Bundy—
>
> If you were referring to Arnold Papadoupoulos, I personally recommended him for an opening which amounted to a promotion for him.
>
>    As the project winds down, we are actively seeking other opportunities for several members of our group.
>
> —Smythe

If an attack is based on insecurity, you might protect your name while stroking your attacker's ego. In this way, you may convince the attacker that you are an ally and discourage him from future forays. Bundy reveals his insecurity by trying to blame Smythe for his own problems.

> Mr. Smythe—
>
> A number of people, myself included, were serious candidates for the position Papadoupoulos just took. You might wait for a more mutually convenient time before flooding the market with your rejects.
>
> —Alex W. Bundy

In his response, Smythe is careful to make no promises, interjecting "may" and "would appear."

> Dear Bundy—
>
> I would not have connected you with the Papadoupoulos spot— your work in lepidopterology would appear to qualify you for the field supervisory post that may be funded toward the end of the year.
>
> —R. S.

An attack based on erroneous information is not really a personal attack, but it still requires a response. Bundy jumps to a faulty conclusion that all computer errors are Smythe's responsibility.

> Mr. Smythe—
>
> Your computer system has completely fouled up the payroll deductions for my department.
>
> —Alex W. Bundy

Smythe corrects Bundy in a cool, straightforward manner.

> Dear Bundy—
>
> Your department is still under the old payroll system—this computer system is only issuing checks to a control group in Finance.
>
> You should contact Mary Milque in payroll to resolve your deduction problems.
>
> —R. S.

In preparation for filing charges against E. F. Hutton, the prosecutor chided Hutton's attorney: "It's been some time since we heard from you." The defense protested:

> To say that "it's been some time since we heard from you" infers lack of cooperation by Hutton in this investigation, and that is not accurate . . .                                        Carpenter, p. 46

A seasoned professional does not allow an important misrepresentation to stand without correction.

# Responding to Valid Criticism

*The best argument is that which seems merely an explanation.*

DALE CARNEGIE

An attack based on valid criticism can be much more difficult to deal with. Approaches from which to choose range from peacemaking to diversion.

*Scenario:* Smythe receives the following memo, a borderline personal attack, from Alberti. Smythe has two problems: the criticisms may be valid, and Alberti is his boss.

> Mr. Smythe—
>
> Regarding the computer project entrusted to your care, it has come to my attention that some serious delays and cost overruns may be in the offing.
>
> In addition, the question has arisen that you may not be taking advantage of the experience and skills of all the staff assigned to this project.

You understand, of course, that my purpose in bringing these problems to the fore is to assure a successful and cost-effective installation of the new system.

—Horatio Alberti

In the responses that follow, Smythe assumes various defensive postures. In each pair of responses, the second offers a stronger defense than the first.

A peacemaking posture suggests a willingness to compromise to avoid conflict. It often starts with a point of agreement.

 Mr. Alberti—

Re: Your memo on computer project

In response to your memo on the computer project, I didn't realize there were so many problems, and I certainly appreciate your concern. What do you think we should do?

—Richard Smythe

Although this memo avoids conflict, it fails to inspire any confidence or address the two questions raised. A stronger response would be:

 Mr. Alberti—

Re: Your memo on computer project

In response to your memo on the computer project, I very much appreciate your concern. Your suggestions are welcome.

As you know, we had a 500 percent increase in cost from the major software supplier, and I am now negotiating the revised contract. I hope to have agreement later this month and do not anticipate a major delay.

I have called a meeting of the entire staff to discuss how we might best take advantage of their experience and skills. I will naturally keep you informed of our progress.

—Richard Smythe

A blaming posture shifts or denies responsibility. There is a fine line between wimping out and denying a statement (or implication) with dignity. Blaming is more likely to raise eyebrows than elicit sympathy, although it may let you off the hook.

 Mr. Alberti—

Re: Your memo on computer project

Those hints you made about my computer project were really unfair.

First of all, you have to realize that the delays were due to the faulty software delivered by the vendor. Secondly, the so-called cost overruns are the responsibility of the people who came up with the original budget. I don't know where they got their numbers, but they sure didn't ask for my opinion.

As for the staff, you have no idea what some of these people are like. Most of them are okay, but some of them, well, you assign them a little work and they run all over the place complaining to anybody who wants to listen. I'm just trying to get them to do their jobs, but I can't do it all for them.

—Richard Smythe

Whatever your posture, a strong defense is one that offers solutions to a problem.

 Mr. Alberti—

Re: Your memo on computer project

You raised two questions about my computer project: costs and personnel.

The cost and schedule overruns may be directly attributed to the original budget and schedule. As I was not involved in this process, I cannot vouch for the numbers or the rationale from which they were derived. However, I believe my revised figures are accurate and am attaching a copy of my budget/schedule notes FYI.

With regard to the staff, the current rash of defections has certainly set us back. We are actively recruiting new professionals while attempting to establish on-site training for those already assigned to the project. Meanwhile, we continue to maximize the resources available to us.

—Richard Smythe

The impersonal and unflappable approach seems to suggest "This is all so matter-of-fact, it has nothing to do with you or me personally."

 Mr. Alberti—

Re: Your memo on computer project

Software problems are just about cleared up and budgets always run a little over on major computer installations.

Staff's okay, but the project could use another tech.

—Smythe

The lack of substance such as numbers detracts from this memo's credibility. Projected costs and a completion date make it more authoritative.

Mr. Alberti—

Re: Your memo on the computer project

The latest projections:
> Software costs: $245,000
> Completion date: September 1997
There is no problem with the staff, but the project could use another tech.

—Smythe

A diversionary or irrelevant response can distract your attacker's attention from the issue he or she raised and which you would prefer not to confront.

 Mr. Alberti—

You sure brought up a lot of interesting points in your memo concerning the computer project, which is moving right along except for the initial software problems, which the vendor said they weren't responsible for due to the last-minute tax changes in the state of Delaware which, in and of themselves, do not affect our organization other than for their impact on the overall system.

I have not heard a great deal about the cost overruns; you're obviously more aware of them since you are on the "inside," so to speak, of all those budget-related matters.

Do you think those staff problems you mentioned might have had to do with the cost overruns or the personnel turnovers in the department? I'll bet you know more of what's going on in terms of personnel than most of the people who work here.

Well, I'm sure glad we've had a chance to explore some of these issues, not that we've necessarily solved all of them to date.

—Richard Smythe

The memo avoids the issue, but it rambles and produces a sense of confusion and incompetence. A more effective diversion offers the appearance of relevance while dodging the main issue.

 Mr. Alberti—

Re: Your memo on the computer project

The schedule and cost overruns to which you referred are in the process of being resolved. It is interesting to note that both are completely compatible for projects of this magnitude. For instance, the latest edition of *Lepidopterology Weekly* has a very interesting analysis of this point. A copy of the article is attached.

In terms of personnel, I am aware that we have lost four good computer people in the last few months. We are trying to strengthen our esprit de corps to fight this. The Holt Corporation has had similar problems, and I have been lunching weekly with my counterpart there. She confirms the commonality of problems which we apparently share with a number of firms in our field.

—Smythe

Confidence may allay worries, as long as it is is not unfounded.

 Mr. Alberti—

Re: Your memo on the computer project

I would like to address the concerns you mentioned, i.e., the questions of delays and cost overruns.

You are no doubt aware of the faulty software originally delivered by the vendor. To those of us in computer systems, such malfunctions are not uncommon and often have potentially advantageous side-effects. For one, they force us to become intimately familiar with the system ahead of schedule. For another, they challenge us to anticipate and resolve problems early on.

As to the "cost overruns," we feel they are really misnomers, because they do not take into consideration the peripherals required for the project, which were not included in the original budget, nor the database administration costs, which should be amortized across several future projects that will share the new database.

The delicate issue of staff problems is probably the result of too many cooks and too few stoves. The very nature of our team presupposes that some talented professionals will occasionally have to roll up their sleeves to share in the tedious, but essential, coding and testing (I do it myself!).

Please let me know if you have any additional questions.

—Richard Smythe

Tightening the writing style can help sell the illusion of confidence.

 Mr. Alberti—

Re: Your memo on the computer project

You know of the faulty software originally delivered by the vendor. The analysts in our group are so accustomed to such malfunctions that we try to use them to our advantage, by becoming intimately familiar with the system ahead of schedule.

The cost overruns are misnomers because they do not take into consideration the peripherals required for the project, which were not included in the original budget, nor the database administration costs, which should be amortized across several future projects that will share the new database.

The delicate issue of staff problems is probably the result of the nature of our team: it presupposes that we all will occasionally have to roll up our sleeves and pitch in.

—Richard Smythe

Alberti's original memo raised two problems: (1) the possible delays and cost overruns and (2) the question of Smythe's talent in the area of personnel. Both of these questions can be satisfactorily addressed by taking any of the defensive postures described. However, combining two or more of these approaches might provide an even stronger response.

Mr. Alberti—
Re: Your memo on computer project

As you know, I inherited this computer project about three months ago and already have identified problems in cost and schedule projections and personnel selection. Here are my current projections:

Latest projection of software costs: $245,000

Latest completion date: September 1997

We have been conducting meetings with the entire staff to discuss how to profit from their experience and skills.

I will naturally keep you informed of progress on all topics.

—Smythe

# 9

# Defending Your Position

*Beware of rashness, but with energy and sleepless*
*vigilance go forward and give us victories.*

ABRAHAM LINCOLN

Your current position may be an important stepping-stone in your career, one you want to protect until you're ready to vacate it. However, your position may be a pawn in an executive's game plan, or a step up in someone else's career path. If your position is threatened, you will need to fortify your place within the hierarchy by analyzing where attacks are coming from and presenting your defense appropriately.

## Analyzing Positional Attacks

*He that will not sail 'till all dangers are over must never*
*put to sea.*

THOMAS FULLER

Companies review task and staff requirements periodically and may shift authority and responsibility from a passive incumbent to a more dynamic employee. More aggressive companies require you to supply "truck memos," asking you to recommend your replacement if you were hit by a truck or otherwise vacated your position.

Your vigilance has to extend in all directions to protect your foothold on the corporate ladder, for positional attacks can come from above, across (your peers), or below (your subordinates).

## Bombshells from Above

*Don't look now, but someone is stealing your potatoes.*

RUSSIAN PROVERB

When executives jockey for position, they often view staff as minor pieces on a chessboard. In chess, a sacrificed pawn may be acceptable; in the game of business, a human pawn—perhaps you or a colleague—may suffer. Executives think little of restructuring a company in order to improve their own positions. During such changes, it is not unusual for positions to be pruned or merged.

If your position is perceived as not essential to the company's main function, management might eliminate you and your entire group during a financial pinch. Special projects and research units with little short-term return on investment can be pruned easily, without even redrawing organization charts.

*Scenario:* Tough financial times have hit Smythe's company. Smythe realizes that his group, which is working on an experimental accounting program, is not secure. The program promises to be cost-effective, but is not quite ready. He receives a memo.

> To:      R. F. Smythe
> From:   Ramona Finch
> Re:       Experimental Accounting Department
>
> In these times of challenge to our company, the decision has been made to limit our commitments. Experimental projects like yours must be put on the back burner until improved profitability allows us to again consider such experiments.
>
> Therefore, please submit to me by the first of the month your summary of the gains that you have made and plans for the relocation or outplacement of your personnel.

The decision to phase out Smythe's program has already been made, making for an uphill battle. Smythe would have found it much easier had he been more effective in bringing Finch onto his side, or developing intelligence sources to provide an early warning.

Instead, Smythe must now present a case to Finch that his program is indeed not experimental, but that it is ready to be implemented and will quickly prove more cost-effective than the existing system.

To:      Ramona Finch
From:   R. F. Smythe
Re:      Experimental Accounting Department

I am pleased to announce that the EAD is indeed operational and will save the company approximately $400,000 per year in accounting costs. The one minor glitch will be corrected by the end of the month.

There are two ways the board can go:

1. They can implement the disbanding of EAD. The current accounting overhead of 12% will continue, and there will be the severance costs for EAD.

2. They can implement the new program and reduce annual costs by $400,000. There will be slightly greater severance costs as many of the traditional accountants are phased out.

Smythe's optimistic response may buy him and his team some time, unless the board recognizes the "minor glitch" as a delaying tactic and goes ahead with disbanding his department.

If your position is duplicated elsewhere in the company, it is subject to being merged with another position to save space and salary. A merger is often a takeover of one group by another, with one group clearly in the driver's seat. Despite pleasant wording, most mergers result in unpleasant reality for the team on the passenger side.

*Scenario:* The following memo has sealed the fate of most of the XYZ group management.

To:      All Personnel
From:   H. McGraw
Re:      Merging of ABC and XYZ Divisions

In these times of challenge to our company, we must make every dollar count toward the day-to-day operations—there is no option but to downsize.

In an effort to gain economies of scale, I have made the decision to merge the ABC and XYZ Divisions.

The new division, called ABX, will maintain both corporate identities and will be a merger in the truest sense.

Mr. Leroi, the general manager of ABC, has accepted the title of Executive Vice President and will head the ABX Division. Reporting to him on a temporary basis will be the five ABC vice presidents, thus keeping together a successful management team.

This memo is a clear-cut announcement that the members of the XYZ division are on their own. Anyone from XYZ receiving this memo must immediately take action, either by hitting the job market before his peers or by trying to ally himself with the conquerors.

*Scenario:* Jack Donaldson, the XYZ business manager, moves to save his position in this takeover.

> To: Rex Leroi, Executive V.P.
> From: Jack Donaldson, XYZ Business Manager
>
> Congratulations on your new position.
> I have been proposing such a merger for some time, and am gratified at the new company structure.
> I look forward to working with you and the ABC business manager—together, we can make ABX a financially sound division.

Donaldson is trying to survive the coup by infiltrating the ranks of the conquerors.

## Encroachment by Peers

> *The defect of equality is that we only desire it with our superiors.*
> HENRY BECQUE

Acquisitive colleagues have been known to recommend to management that elements of someone else's position would be better housed in their domain. One way to foil such an attempt to encroach is to magnify the potential ramifications of the proposed shake-up. The idea will be dropped if management anticipates the change would complicate matters and create more problems than it would solve.

*Scenario:* I. B. Grabbe tries to extend his power by implementing a procedure for his peers. If no one contests it, he will have established a measure of de facto control.

> To: Staff
> From: I. B. Grabbe, Associate Chief, Budget
>
> So that the funds needed for essential operations remain available throughout the fiscal year, it has been suggested that unbudgeted expenses in excess of $100 be authorized in writing both by the

corresponding department head (as is currently the case) and by the chief or associate chief of budgeting.

To facilitate this procedure, a new form has been proposed by this department (copy of proposed Form 718X–9b attached).

Arnold takes swift action to neutralize the move. He stresses the ramifications in a memo to the key decision maker, and forwards copies to the other department heads.

> To: General Manager
> From: Arnold Papadoupoulos
>
> As you know, the current procedure allows for a quick response in a competitive environment. To the best of our knowledge, this flexibility has never been abused.
>
> Mr. Grabbe's suggestion would require authorization at two levels. This would:
>
> 1. remove authority from those doing the negotiating,
>
> 2. tie their hands when searching for creative solutions, and
>
> 3. impose an unproductive and unneeded bureaucratic step.
>
> The supposed benefit is to add an unnecessary safeguard. A better solution might be to replace those whom you've decided are not competent to exercise authority.

Arnold has effectively exposed Grabbe's effort as a thinly disguised power grab to the manager who has the power to stop it. He also has exposed the attempt to the other department heads.

## Competition from Below

> *We hope that, when the insects take over the world, they will remember with gratitude how we took them along on all our picnics.*
>
> BILL VAUGHAN

Talented subordinates may try to push you up or out to clear a foothold for themselves. If you're not interested in moving aside, you've got to protect against their encroachment.

*Scenario:* Tina Upman, the assistant chief of budget, is aiming at a promotion that would elevate her to the same corporate level as her boss, Grabbe.

> To:    B. B. O'Boile, Deputy Controller
> From:  Tina Upman, Assistant Chief, Budget
>
> I would like to confirm my willingness to assume the responsibilities of an associate chief.
>
> With Mr. Grabbe already overloaded with responsibilities, it seems an excellent division of labor to assign to me the field budgeting responsibilities for which (I am told) I am being considered. You may recall that I was a field supervisor prior to joining Budget. The upgrade of my current position to that of associate chief would give me the credibility to represent the field staff and would bring a younger voice to the budget meetings.

Grabbe knows that there are three good ways to protect yourself from subordinates. One is to nurture and direct them.

> To:    B. B. O'Boile, Deputy Controller
> From:  I. B. Grabbe, Associate Chief, Budget
>
> Budgeting responsibilities for the field staff is naturally a function of this office and is growing in importance.
>
> I therefore recommend the promotion of Tina Upman as a specialist in field staff budgeting. We can work together, Tina gaining from my experience and my gaining from her knowledge of computerized cost control.

Another way to defend yourself from climbers is to offer them your enthusiastic support—along a career path outside your sphere of interest.

> To:    Tina Upman, Assistant Chief, Budget
> From:  I. B. Grabbe, Associate Chief, Budget
>
> An opening for which you would be uniquely suited is about to materialize in Finance. The position is currently classified as an assistant chief, but will be upgraded to associate chief as soon as the division has been adequately staffed.
>
> If you're interested, I'm behind you all the way!

A third, but drastic, alternative to fending off subordinates is to crush them. Bear in mind, however, that today's subordinate may be tomorrow's supervisor.

> To:    T. Upman
> From:  I. B. Grabbe
>
> As senior member of this department, I feel called upon to remind

you of the need for all of us to pull together in fulfilling our responsibilities.

While individual initiative is no less encouraged here than throughout the corporation, it is important to distinguish between actions that are independent of team efforts and those that may impact on the group in a negative manner.

# Identifying the Jury

*The hardest thing to learn in life is which bridge to cross and which to burn.*

DAVID RUSSELL

Aggressors attacking your position are likely to seek support from someone higher than you on the corporate ladder.

*Scenario:* Arnold gave Burt an unreasonable deadline and a strongly worded memo that hinted that Burt's job was on the line. Burt overreacted.

> To:       Arnold
> From:   Burt
>
> Your memo wasn't fair at all. I can't possibly finish the report this week, since the figures won't be available from the controller's office until next week.
>
> When I showed your memo to the controller, he agreed there was no way it could be done before the end of next week, and that he was going to take care of everything.
>
> Then I showed your memo to the head attorney, and he assured me that you couldn't fire me for something that wasn't my fault.
>
> Next I showed it to the CFO, who told me not to worry, that she would talk to you.

Better judgment would have cautioned Burt to stop after seeing the controller. Showing Arnold's memo to the others was overkill. Aside from making Arnold very angry, Burt has begun to wear out the welcome mat upstairs. After all, he can't go to these people every time he has a problem. What happens if he really needs their support some day?

*Scenario:* When Austin Duff was appointed group vice president, David Freuh became general manager. David quickly promoted Adam Sennic to take his place.

As vice president of Product Development, Sennic attempts to encroach on Robyn Leigh and the Marketing Department.

> To:     David Freuh, General Manager
> From:   Adam Sennic, V.P., Product Development
> Re:     Restructuring of Product Development
>
> As we discussed, I want to formally recommend that the market research function currently handled by Marketing be shifted to Product Development.
>
> While not a major issue, it would eliminate headaches in Marketing (which is not trained in research techniques) and would be of help to us in Product Development.

Robyn obtains a copy of this memo and now must decide how to respond to Adam's aggression. She realizes that Adam was promoted by Freuh, that they have discussed this matter, and that Freuh is likely to side with Adam. She also know that judgment by an antagonistic jury could result in the loss of her case and possibly her job. Although she reports to Freuh, Robyn must appeal to someone else to seek a more satisfactory outcome.

Austin Duff, the new group vice president, seems appropriate. As Freuh's supervisor, he could neutralize Adam's attempt at encroachment. Robyn believes that Austin respects her work, so she addresses her appeal to him.

> To:     Austin Duff, Group Vice President
> From:   Robyn Leigh, V.P., Marketing
> Re:     Sennic Memo on Restructuring of Product Development
>
> Attached is a copy of Adam Sennic's memo recommending a restructuring of the Product Development and Marketing departments.
>
> I do not agree with his suggestions and would like your guidance in responding. Can we meet on Thursday so that I can get your input?

The ideal jury is the one that is favorable to you and has the power to make and enforce a decision.

# Presenting Your Defense

*It is not so much in holding a good hand as playing a poor hand well.*

H. T. LESLIE

Once you have accepted a judge and done all you can to ensure a fair hearing, decide how best to present your defense. There are three options: respond to the attack; launch a completely separate counterattack; or introduce a red herring.

*Scenario:* Robyn responds to Adam's encroachment by attacking his proposal and supporting her own position.

> To:     Austin Duff, Group Vice President
> From:   Robyn Leigh, V.P. Marketing
> Re:     Proposed restructure
>
> I disagree with the idea that the market research function currently handled by my department be shifted to Product Development.
>
> Marketing research is indeed a specialized function, and we were very lucky to add Pam Amherst—a trained market researcher—to our staff. She not only has contributed to our sales results, but has systematically fed product information to the Product Development group on my recommendation. It is worth noting that both of Adam Sennic's associates have commended Pam on her help in developing product profiles.
>
> Frankly, marketing research uses concepts and language foreign to Product Development people and provides information that would not be understood by traditional developers. The only way that MR would work here is to give Pam a supportive home in Marketing and use a person like Jim Owen to translate her work for Adam.
>
> Market research is the eyes and ears of the Marketing department. Since your approval of this function when you were the general manager, sales have increased from $75 million to $100 million.
>
> I disagree with Adam Sennic—$25,000,000 most certainly IS a major issue.

*Scenario:* Instead of limiting herself to Adam's attack, Robyn could decide to propose her own plan. In this counterattack, Robyn ignores

Adam's attack and launches her own initiative. If she is successful, she'll become Adam's boss.

> To:      Austin Duff, Group Vice President
> From:   Robyn Leigh, V.P. Marketing
> Re:      Proposed restructure
>
> Proctor & Gamble has been organized by product teams under the management of a product manager. The head of Tide, for example, is a marketer with responsibility for marketing, manufacturing, and product development.
>
> Recently, many large companies have adopted this structure (see attached articles from *Industry Week*). I believe this structure will work here, with the benefits of reduced costs, lower failure rates with new products, and vastly increased profits. Note the summary on page 34—"in 23 companies which have adopted this organizational structure, 21 have increased profits by at least 7% within 2 years."
>
> Can we schedule a brief meeting next week to discuss how to proceed?

As an alternative, you may be able to introduce a red herring that obscures the issue by redirecting attention or introducing so much extraneous information that the jury will never get around to making a decision.

*Scenario:* The following memo, from Time Warner's vice chairman to its chairman, was written ostensibly to encourage a merger, but its underlying aim seems to be to delay action. A memo can pretend to aim at resolving an issue while its real objective may be to stir up disagreement and confusion.

> To:      J. Richard Munro
> From:   Gerald M. Levin
> Date:   August 11, 1987
>
> I am now convinced that our primary objective should be merger. Like IBM or GE its size and range of solid franchises would make it an institutional "must carry" stock. The combination could be accomplished through a no premium merger, shareholder value would be enhanced without the insanely pricey dilution so prevalent in the purchase of assets today. . . .
>
> As we saw with Gannett [newspaper group], the potential asset combination can be compelling in theory but meaningless in the real

world if the cultures are incompatible or the CEOs cannot relate. . . . A word of caution and reality:  neither our senior management nor our board will presently proceed to the end result I have described. The memorandum is intended to provoke debate and not detail the mechanics.                                                      Clurman, pp. 151, 152

# 10

## Preemptive Measures

*He who excels at resolving difficulties does so before*
*they arise.*

SUN TZU

One of the most time-consuming and dangerous pastimes in business is trying to beat off personal or positional attacks. Such efforts win no laurels and most often are in lose-lose situations. Unless you wish to spend time extinguishing fires, take preemptive action to eliminate attacks from managers, peers, and subordinates before they occur.

## Preventing Attacks from On High

*Everyone who achieves . . . had a mentor, someone to*
*whose spark of encouragement and teaching he owes his*
*achievement.*

VERASWAMI

The two most common forms of attack from above are through pruning and merging. In both cases, it helps to tie your position to a strong manager who has the resources to protect your operation.

Mentors can teach you tricks of the trade, help keep you out of trouble, run interference for you, and take you with them as they go up the ladder or across the street. The value of cultivating a mentor, or sponsor, cannot be overestimated. They can defend you in your absence, promote your point of view, and gain you access to avenues that might otherwise be dead ends. It's difficult to win without an experienced coach.

Developing a mentor relationship requires persuading your target of your loyalty, your willingness to share your grapevine, and your readiness to roll up your sleeves and help when asked.

*Scenario:* Hugh decides that B. B. O'Boile might make a good mentor. O'Boile has ready access to Flexor, the controller, and appears pleasant and sharp. Hugh reads in the company newsletter that B. B. is working on a special project to increase productivity by adopting an E-mail system. He recognizes that this is an excellent opportunity to get to know O'Boile, and vice versa, and sends him this note.

> To:       B. B. O'Boile
> From:   Hugh
>
> I understand you are exploring E-mail systems and thought that some of my research and personal files of related articles might be of interest (attached).
>      In particular, you might want to read the *Computer World* article—excuse the highlighting of what I considered valuable comments.
>      If you're developing a team to evaluate and set up an E-mail system, I'd like to volunteer.

Hugh is offering to apprentice himself to B. B. If B. B. accepts the offer, they will develop a symbiotic relationship where B. B. will nurture, protect, and teach, while Hugh will work hard to learn the lessons and become a valuable adjunct to O'Boile.

The initial area of mutual interest is a companywide project that will allow Hugh to network with people whom he would not otherwise meet. The mutual goal would be to expand this relationship—to make it an ongoing one where Hugh learns B. B.'s skills and B. B. gains a new right hand.

Even if this growth does not occur, Hugh is still able to make the following claim.

> In addition to my normal responsibilities, I've been working with Mr. O'Boile on a project assigned by Mr. Flexor.

If O'Boile declines a personal interest in protecting Hugh, at least Hugh has identified himself as an interested employee who reads the company's house organ and doesn't shirk from extra work.

# Preventing Attacks from Peers

*One must be a fox to recognize traps, and a lion to frighten wolves.*

NICCOLO MACHIAVELLI

Prevention may prove effective in three areas of possible conflict with your peers: if you and someone else are both committed to plans of action; if you are committed to a plan of action and your peer is committed to the status quo; and if you are committed to the status quo and your peer is committed to a plan of action.

A peer who is committed to a plan of action—even one contrary to yours—is a potential ally: you may have common obstacles to overcome. Try to bring this colleague into your camp, through salesmanship, redirection, or cutting a deal.

To sell your idea, you must persuade your colleague that your plan is at least as good or is more likely to succeed. Remember, your goal is to make an ally.

> Rick—
>
> The company would profit from E-mail to improve efficiency.
> I understand that you are inclined toward using temps.
>
> My research suggests that E-mail is cost-effective and has a solid chance of being implemented due to space and head-count limitations.
>
> Let's get together for lunch and discuss these issues. I would very much like to have you on my side.
> —Hugh

If you cannot sell your idea, try to redirect your colleague to an area which is less threatening to your position.

> Rick—
>
> Your idea about bringing in some word-processing temps overlooks our lack of space. We've barely enough room for the existing staff.
>
> On the other hand, there is a real need for training the existing secretaries in the area of supervision or training them to handle it themselves.
> —Hugh

Referring to a plan as an *idea* reduces its stature; *proposal* is reserved for your own plans.

If a sales pitch and redirection don't work, try to cut a deal. Hugh's ace in the hole is his connection with O'Boile.

> Rick—
>
> I recognize that you favor the use of temps, while I remain committed to E-mail. Either way, O'Boile's support is needed for approval.
>
> Let's get together for lunch and discuss our mutual interests— perhaps we can join forces.
>
> —Hugh

Ridiculing a plan without offering alternatives will be construed as a personal attack. To avoid making an enemy, begin with a supportive statement, provide options, and keep your tone constructive. If you can't convince your colleague to adopt your concept or reach a compromise, you have an adversary who may attack you or your position in the future. Keep track of his activities.

If your colleague prefers the status quo over your plan to bring about some change, you are facing a potential bottleneck. Be patient and apply easy pressure on the obstruction: too much pressure and a bottleneck becomes intransigent. Allow a way out; as Sun Tzu advised, "Do not thwart an enemy returning homewards." Also read Chapter 13 on uncorking bottlenecks.

If you are committed to the status quo and your colleague has a plan for change, *you* may be perceived as the bottleneck. Unless opponents see you as inflexible or intransigent, they are not likely to attack. If you are willing to bend, even a radical adversary may be appeased. Again, read Chapter 13 for strategies.

## Preventing Attacks from Below

> *By working faithfully eight hours a day, you may
> eventually get to be a boss and work twelve hours a day.*
>
> ROBERT FROST

Ambitious subordinates push upward to carve niches for themselves. You can protect yourself through nurturing, a long-term preventive measure that may bear substantial returns.

Aside from experiencing the satisfaction of helping someone deserving get ahead, you can gain a loyal subordinate who may be entrusted with confidential tasks, inform you about what's going on in other departments, and protect your back at each rung up the corporate ladder.

*Scenario:* Grabbe provides Tina with constructive criticism and enough positive reinforcement to encourage her allegiance.

> Dear Tina—
>
> I was impressed by your report on reorganization and will do all I can to promote your views.
>
> Before I forward this report, however, I suggest that you analyze the underlying statistics (especially those on page 4, which seem to contradict the ones on page 6).
>
> Also, you should be aware that the strongest emotion in these halls is reverence for the bottom line—see if you can rework your conclusions to appeal to the bean counters among us.
>
> In bean-counter terminology, I would say that the bottom line on you is "in the black." I'm pleased with your work and enjoy helping you make a name for yourself.
>
> —I. B. Grabbe

Assign your Young Turks extra work if it would be useful to you— they're willing to invest some overtime for their future. Guide them through the intricacies of the job and of the company. If your mentoring is personal and effective, your subordinates will loyally come back to you for help and guidance.

# The CYA

*A memorandum is written not to inform the reader but to protect the writer.*

DEAN ACHESON

The CYA (cover your ass) memo is a way of protecting your posterior against potential damage by going on record with your position. CYAs can be used to let people know what you have done, are now doing, or intend to do, so they can't later claim that they would have objected had they known. If a firm warns its clients about anticipated charges, the clients are less apt to protest when an invoice arrives.

> Mr. Paypay,
>
> I shall be spending between 100 and 200 hours researching your case this week (all hours in excess of 35 per week are billed at double, while hours in excess of 40 are billed at triple).
>
> Yours sincerely,
>
> Winford Sterling
> Nickel, Dime, Quarter, Sawbuck, and Dollar, Esq.

The memo you write today may be used against you someday. Incautious statements are potentially dangerous because of the way they may be interpreted, in or out of context, by future readers. Try to word your CYA vaguely enough so that you can interpret it later as pro, con, or ambivalent.

> Mr. Sterling—
>
> Being a team player, I prefer not to "go against the flow." Thus my views with regard to Project Flimflam are based to a greater degree on the recommendation of the Executive Committee than on thorough familiarity with or a personal commitment to the financial projections contained in the proposal.
>
> —N. Paypay

*Scenario:* Nelson is in charge of Marketing. George, the head of Product Development, asks Nelson's opinion about releasing a new chewing gum. George reports an unpleasant side effect: the gum may abrade dentures, although the process seems slow enough to make it difficult for anyone to blame the gum.

Despite Nelson's sense of responsibility to customers, he needs a new product to improve revenues. Nelson, using George's familiarity with the topic, drafts a list of statements ranging from incriminating to innocuous.

> I believe we should:
> 1. release the gum for sale despite the uncertain lab results.
> 2. release the product for sale.
> 3. allow the product to be released for sale unless there are any negative lab results.
> 4. delay the product pending further confirmation of our encouraging lab results.

Next Nelson focuses on how to express his opinion. His phrases become increasingly vague.

1. I concur that we should . . .
2. I am aware of no reason not to . . .
3. Based on the materials you provided, I am inclined to agree with you that there is no reason not to . . .
4. But for the denture question, there would seem to be no reason preventing us from . . .

Nelson chooses to take a positive but nonincriminating stance.

George—

Based on the materials you provided, I am inclined to agree with you that there is no reason not to release the product for sale, unless there are any negative lab results which have not been brought to my attention.

—Nelson

George knows that Nelson is familiar with the lab test that reported the abraded dentures (which Nelson was careful not to mention in his memo), and he assumes that Nelson has considered it in his decision to support the product. Years later, Nelson can always claim that he was unaware of any negative tests, as long as he has not signed off on the report in writing or kept a copy of it in his files.

For his part, George could protect himself by filing a copy of Nelson's memo with the lab report. At a future date, he could reasonably insist that, to his understanding, Nelson's memo was contingent on the report.

When possible, support your memos with any available corroborative documents (attach them to your filed copy). Some people create and file copies of MMs in which they question the wisdom of a decision—without forwarding the original to the addressee. They also make sure there are no contradictory documents in their files.

# Creating History

*History is never anything more than an imaginative reconstruction of the past.*

ORSON SCOTT CARD

Businesses thrive on record keeping to maintain continuity and direction. Your memos record your unique interpretation of what occurred and what was intended.

## Taking Minutes

*Never let the other fellow set the agenda.*

JAMES BAKER

An opportunity unfolds every time you meet with others—to plan, summarize, or discuss an issue—to apply your version of reality to the meeting by taking its minutes. Minutes become the permanent record etched into posterity against fading recollections. If you take and polish them, then your interpretations become the official annals. Obviously you won't falsify what happened at the meeting, but you might expand on the issues that are important to you.

*Scenario:* Roger Bincheeling works for a company that is developing a new accounts receivable system. He volunteers to take the minutes at the weekly status meetings. This gets him invited to all status meetings and gives him additional exposure to the managers of Systems Development and Accounts Receivable, each of whom has a different opinion of the project. Systems Development believes that Accounts Receivable is changing system requirements. Accounts Receivable accuses Systems Development of misunderstanding their needs.

If Roger were partial to Systems Development, he could protect their interest by including their concern.

> It was pointed out that additional changes to the original user requirements were likely to result in cost overrides and delays in the deliverable dates.

If Roger were to favor Accounts Receivable, his summary could reflect that department's criticism of the potential system.

> It was suggested that an analysis be made at this stage to assure that the new system will accurately and thoroughly provide essential business functionality.

## Making Notes

*One place where you're sure to find the perfect driver is in the back seat.*

HOMER PHILLIPS

If there is an official recorder whose job you are unable to usurp, make notes on the points that interest you, record them in more detail than the designated scribe would, and ask to review and supplement his minutes. He might be glad to include your notes, because they will make his own record look more complete. If the minutes are taken by someone who rejects your offer, you're limited to providing your observations on a single subject or two every now and then.

Alternatively, you might summarize your recollection of a particular point in an MM to your boss. If accepted, copy the other involved parties.

> The committee chairperson recommended that Systems Development and Accounts Receivable conduct a study to weigh potential cost overrides and delays against essential functionality.

## For the Record

*No one ever listened himself out of a job.*
CALVIN COOLIDGE

For any significant conversation or meeting, you may want to write a contemporaneous account for your own records. These personal minutes will serve to refresh your memory and can be used to protect yourself against someone else's interpretation of the same event.

> Had lunch with Nelson re: marketing plans for new dental product. Expressed reservations about possible abrasive quality. Judgment is not mine on this point.

*Scenario:* Hugh meets with Burt and Felicia to plan how to convince Arnold to order state-of-the-art computers. They agree to drop certain hints and to meet again to intensify the campaign. Hugh writes a memo to himself.

> Me: Talk about smaller footprint of newer machines, networking capability.
>
> Him: Remind him to stress cost savings through increased speed and storage efficiency.
>
> Her: Remind her to get on his case.

*Scenario:* Louis Buchalter, alias Louis Lepke, was the highest-level crime syndicate leader ever to be executed in the electric chair. Realizing that his family would not long survive him if the mob believed that he had ratted, he dictated this last-minute note to his wife, who read it to the press.

I am anxious to have it clearly understood that I did not offer to talk and give information in exchange for any promise of commutation of my death sentence. I did not ask that!    Sifakis, pp. 185–88, 312

By having his wife publicize the memo, Lepke was reassuring the syndicate that he hadn't squealed and that his family should be protected.

# Building an Empire

*Having it all doesn't mean having it all at once.*
STEPHANIE LUETKEHANS

Bureaucrats tend to evaluate success in terms of numbers, especially head count and budget responsibilities. The more people in your department, the more apparent power you have. Bottom liners juggle their desire to expand against their need to control costs to protect their own positions, so empire building becomes a major preoccupation.

Claiming the need for more personnel and larger expense budgets without increasing a return on the company's investment is harder to justify.

*Scenario:* Roz was asked to submit her budget for the upcoming fiscal year. She justified her requests in a cover memo.

To:    Clark
From:    Roz

Our staffing and budgetary needs for the coming fiscal year are attached. Please note that staffing is identical to last year and includes the addition of the two positions we gave up during the rollbacks.

The marketing budget calls for an additional $47 million which, as a percentage of gross sales and factoring in the inflation figures issued by the government last month, represents a virtual increase of only 1.3 percent and is in fact 0.7 percent lower than projected growth rates.

By redefining one's charter or repositioning one's product, empire building can be very profitable for the company. Telephone companies recognized the need to become communication networks or go the way of railroads that failed to consider themselves in the transportation business.

*Scenario:* Randy supervises the book department of a large department store chain. After several customers requested the audio version of a best-selling title and left unable to make their purchases, Randy uses the opportunity to persuade the store manager to expand the book realm.

> To:     Mr. Howard
> From:   Randy
>
> In the last three weeks, 22 customers have asked for the audio version of books we carry and 31 have asked for motivational tapes.
>     I need your approval of the attached purchase order to stock these items that would have resulted in over $1000 in sales.

Corporate experience yields several lessons:

- Always ask for more than you need. Your request is assumed to be exaggerated and is likely to be slashed. Request enough so that you may be left with close to what you really need.

- Bear in mind the "boy who cried wolf." If your demands are excessive, frequent, and unfounded, they're likely to be rejected. And frequent rejection of your requests will lead eventually to rejection of you.

- Although everybody's doing it, everybody else is watching. To avoid personal attacks, treat this process with the same subtlety you would devote to anything that may arouse suspicion or jealousy.

Re: # Offense

*In other words, a good offense wins.*
Dan Quayle

We gain control by initiating action rather than waiting for something to happen. Whatever we may want, the written word—the pen or keyboard rather than the sword—is clearly the tool of choice. There are offensive tactics wonderfully suited for manipulation by memo.

# 11

## The Siege

*If you get up early, work late, and pay your taxes, you will get ahead if you strike oil.*

J. PAUL GETTY

Many people need time to adjust to new and unexpected ideas. Some react by automatically pointing their thumbs down when faced with unfamiliar concepts and firmly close their minds when pressed. But even when their initial reaction to a suggestion is negative, they may yet come around if skillfully and patiently coaxed.

Traditional, conservative, and downright stubborn people require special handling, as do some open-minded colleagues. When making reasonable requests of unreasonable people, or unreasonable requests of both reasonable and unreasonable people, you're apt to meet with some resistance. To overcome this inconvenience, we've borrowed from ancient warfare the tactic called the siege.

The siege is a campaign over time. It is useful when a single action or memo is unlikely to bring about your goal. You can apply siege tactics when confronting someone whose immediate reaction to any idea tends to be negative or when presenting an innovative plan, or one that appears risky or self-serving.

The siege can be effective only when your target has the power to approve your request.

*Scenario:* Paul is in the antiques business and he'd like to induce his boss Harriet to let him attend an obscure numismatics conference to be held on the island of Bermuda next November. He's assessed the probability as small, but definitely worth a shot. The siege appears to be his only chance. He begins with an innocent "feeler" to which his unsuspecting supervisor has no reason to object.

> To:      Harriet
> From:   Paul
> Did you read about the old coins that a collector bought for next to nothing down in Mexico? They turned out to be worth a small fortune.
>       Journal article attached FYI.

> To:      Paul
> From:   Harriet
> Thanks for the article about the Incan coins. Very interesting.

Having met with the barest crumb of interest, Paul proceeds.

> To:      Harriet
> From:   Paul
> Further to the article about the Incan coins, the Japanese have found some ceremonial masks adorned with precious stones on the island of Cheju. Isn't it amazing that some of the pieces are actually being auctioned off? Too bad it's so far away.

> To:      Paul
> From:   Harriet
> Yes, it certainly is amazing that the Cheju masks are being sold. Of course, it's halfway around the world.

So far, so good. He's captured her interest without raising her suspicions. He continues.

> To:      Harriet
> From:   Paul
> Have you seen this article about the large number of shipwrecks off the coast of Bermuda?

> To:      Paul
> From:   Harriet
> Appreciate your sharing the article about the Bermuda shipwrecks. Do they have anything to do with the Bermuda Triangle?

Her query is no more than idle curiosity, but at least she's willing to chat along open lines of communication. Paul waits a few weeks before sending another memo, this one attached to a clipping from a creditable journal.

> To:     Harriet
> From:  Paul
>
> I thought it might be a good idea to be on the lookout for precious metals. Collectors have been gobbling them up since the recession took hold. See attached article.

> To:     Paul
> From:  Harriet
>
> It never hurts to watch for bargains.

The positive tone of her response encourages Paul to move ahead more boldly.

> To:     Harriet
> From:  Paul
>
> I certainly agree with you about watching for bargains. But they're getting harder to find around here. Maybe we should expand our search a bit.

> To:     Paul
> From:  Harriet
>
> With profit margins having grown so narrow, we really can't afford to go out on any wild goose chases. What did you have in mind?

Paul realizes his boss is beginning to grow suspicious, so he diverts her attention to avoid a possible rejection. His next memo raises a completely different issue which they are certain to agree on.

> To:     Harriet
> From:  Paul
>
> Considering the effects of the economy on our business, I'd like to explore some ways of increasing the efficiency of our shipping department, including the possibility of staff reductions.

There are two main reasons for his abrupt diversion. First, he wants to evade Harriet's budding demurral on exotic travel before it becomes a full-blown objection. As long as she hasn't turned him down, the game goes on. Since she cannot burst his bubble until she knows about it, Paul is careful not to reveal his plan until she seems more receptive. He cleverly avoids a confrontation until he can improve the odds.

His other motive is to reinforce a pattern of agreement, which Paul wants to encourage—no matter what the issue. The more his views appear in harmony with hers, the more likely she will give him the benefit of any doubt.

> To:      Paul
> From:   Harriet
> Excellent idea. I'll be looking forward to your report.

She has agreed; he has a mandate for his investigations.

Without committing himself to paper, he chats with the Shipping staff to find out what might be done. They tell him what they can, he comes up with useful if not earth-shattering information, and he makes his recommendations accordingly.

> To:      Harriet
> From:   Paul
> I've found a way to cut back on shipping costs and handling without making any staff reductions.

> To:      Paul
> From:   Harriet
> Good job. Let me know what this will translate to in cost reductions.

Paul contributes a modest improvement, no one has to be dismissed, and the chief seems happy with his conclusions. Well and good, but he's no closer to his junket. What now? He carefully composes his next memo, drawing momentum from her most recent agreement.

> To:      Harriet
> From:   Paul
> Between now and next November, we should realize a savings of at least $14,000. I might have some ideas about applying up to half of that amount toward acquiring some potentially high-profit merchandise.

He's finally revealed his big plan. Her response will guide his next step.

If she doesn't respond, he might try another variation. If she responds with something like the following, he can dust off his suitcase and confront her, face-to-face.

> I'd like to hear your ideas when you get a chance.

If her response is not as positive, his efforts still haven't cost him much.

> I think we would be better served to look for some more ways to reduce costs.

At worst, Paul has managed to associate himself with bottom-line efficiency in a period of economic sensitivity. He may even have saved his own job.

# 12
## Stacking the Deck

*When in doubt, win the trick.*

EDMOND HOYLE

Stacking the deck amounts to limiting someone's options to your predefined parameters. This is done by squeezing your target with a straightforward either-or choice or by boxing in your target with more narrowly defined boundaries via a series of diminishing options. The bottom line in stacking the deck is to never—never—allow your target to make the choice you don't want him to make.

## Squeezing

*Even if you're on the right track, you'll get run over if you just sit there.*

WILL ROGERS

The squeeze provides license to control under the guise of being thorough and taking the initiative. It limits your target's choices to your choices. Obviously, your target doesn't have to accept your limits, but why reduce your odds by mentioning an option not to your liking?

Avoid questions that equally invite a yes or no response.

👎 Can I expect my salary increase to go into effect by the beginning of next month?

👎 Do you think I should go to Osaka this month?

A better approach is to encourage your target to chose between two positive responses.

👍 Will my salary increase go into effect this pay period or the first of next month?

👍 Shall I go to Osaka this week, or next week?

With an open-ended question or request, you put yourself in the position of having to wait for a response which may or may not be forthcoming.

👎 Please let me know by the first of the month.

👎 I'll need your totals before the next sales meeting.

Force the issue by ultimatum. Rephrase your memo so that a delayed response or no response will justify your action.

👍 Unless I hear from you by next Wednesday, I'll move ahead with our plan.

👍 In case you don't have enough time to prepare for the orientation program next month, I'd be glad to run it for you. To do this, I need a little more elbow room—I'll move temporarily into that vacant cubicle near your office on Friday morning.

In most cases, the choices we offer are relatively positive. However, there are also situations that are not unlike blackmail:

👎 Don—

There's no way the Accounts Receivable system can be up and running on time to bill for June collectibles unless you authorize virtually unlimited overtime for myself and my team, for the rest of this month and May.

—J. W.

👍 Don—

The schedule on the Accounts Receivable system can only be met by authorizing overtime. As Accounts Receivable and cost containment are both key goals, I assume that overtime for my team for the next two months is acceptable with the proviso that we try to limit these costs.

—J. W.

If you are willing to take risks, hoist your target on his own petard by quoting him.

 When you promised "no new taxes," Mr. President, you won my enthusiastic support.  The increases you recently announced appear to contradict your pledge.  They won't apply to me, will they?

This technique can backfire if you make it easy for the target to refute his words.  The president might be pressured into giving an answer that you don't want.

 Don—
At last month's Board meeting, you said that the schedule on the Accounts Receivable system was "our highest priority."
With this in mind, I have authorized overtime for my team for the next two months, the only way in which we can maintain the schedule.
I will try to limit these costs.
—J. W.

J. W. has stacked the deck by taking action.  Don's canceling of that action would embarrass him in front of the board.  By stacking the deck, J. W. will be able to pursue his initiative.  Don will have to live with the promise of "limiting the costs."

# Boxing In

*. . . One can either do this or that . . . do it or do not do it—you will regret both.*

SØREN KIERKEGAARD

Boxing in consists of maneuvering your target into a corner that is, effectively, a box.  Then you offer a way out, which turns into a smaller box. The objective is to control by successively shrinking your target's options before he can free himself.  Boxing in extends the squeezing tactic and incorporates some siege techniques as well.

*Scenario:* Niko is a new hire in the computer section of Boulder Insurance ("Why settle for a piece of the rock, when you can have a Boulder?").  He desperately wants to distinguish himself from the four other systems programmers in his office. His plan is to position himself in the fast lane by promoting client-server technology, which is as yet unknown at Boulder.

Niko uses an opportunity to access someone on the executive level to sell his technical background—and himself. Rusty, the director of sales and an executive vice president, is impressed with this attentive new hire who seems able to apply new technology to Rusty's needs. Niko borrows some leverage from the executive vice president as he composes a memo to his boss Hazel.

> To:　　Hazel
> cc:　　Rusty
> From:　Niko
>
> As you asked, I got the alternative-format information from Rusty.
> While with him, I mentioned how he could set up his own formats in Lotus using a graphic user interface (GUI). He was especially enthusiastic about the quick turnaround if this were made possible at Boulder.
> I told him it could be easily implemented if existing programming uses a modular information processing (MIPS) approach. He seemed very interested and asked if our programming was developed with MIPS. I told him that the insurance/actuarial tables were definitely *not*, but that some of the sales and payroll programs were partially developed with MIPS in mind.
> I promised to review the entire programming development library (with special reference to sales) and get back to him in about two weeks.
> Is this okay with you? Unless I hear differently, I'll proceed with Rusty's request.

Hazel's options are limited—she can go along with the planned action or can upset the applecart by going head-on against an executive vice president's request. There is not much of a choice—Niko is free to pursue his chosen path.

> To:　　Rusty
> cc:　　Hazel
> From:　Niko
>
> The new payroll and purchasing systems recently developed under Hazel's leadership are in MIPS format. A graphic user interface (GUI) could be put in place within a month, allowing you to set up your own formats.

The actuarial data would necessitate a total overhaul to convert to MIPS. This could be a blessing—for instance, Prudential has moved in this direction and claims that data retrieval is quicker, easier, and more meaningful to the user.

Sales-by-market information is already well along with MIPS, but cross-references to territory and sales staff are traditionally programmed.

You really should see a GUI in action before making any decision. The only working GUI in marketing that I know of is at Pru. I am attaching an article by a friend who set up their system. If you and Hazel would like, I'll talk to him about showing us his work.

With this memo and the article, Niko has supplied useful information and moved both Rusty and Hazel toward a commitment in his chosen direction.

Niko sends the memo just before leaving for a night class. On the following morning, before Rusty or Hazel can respond, he follows up with another memo to keep the ball rolling.

> To:      Hazel
> cc:      Rusty
> From:   Niko
>
> My friend at Pru was in my class last night. I told him about Rusty's and your interest in graphic user interface, and he agreed to show us an operational GUI in marketing.
>
> I'll set up a GUI demo in payroll to let Rusty see what it can do. Meanwhile, my friend has invited us to Pru to review their work and to meet with some of his marketing people who are using the GUI.
>
> Would lunch on Monday the 14th or the 21st be more convenient? Your choice.

Both Hazel and Rusty check their calendars. Neither of them recognizes that Niko is going ahead with the demonstration in payroll: their silence gives Niko tacit approval to proceed. He will try to arrange the lunch, which could be very useful, but he has already accomplished his own goal: to become the company's ombudsman in client-server technology.

Niko is boxing in the area in which to implement a GUI. He continues to borrow leverage effectively: from his friend if the meeting at Pru comes off; from the head of payroll on the GUI demonstration; from Rusty when the implementation becomes a reality; and potentially from Hazel when she makes a commitment to this technology. Niko has played his hand with skill, aggressively making important decisions and allowing others inconsequential choices (like when to go to lunch).

In the following weeks, Niko works with the head of payroll, keeps Rusty and Hazel informed, and otherwise maintains a low profile. Finally, he is able to announce a solid result.

> To:      Hazel
> [bcc:    Rusty]
> From:   Niko
>
> Thanks to your support and backing, the payroll GUI is now operational. A copy of the letter from the head of payroll to the Chairman is attached. I believe that everyone involved in using the graphic user interface is very pleased, and the cost was minimal.
>
> To keep this innovative and cost-effective approach in motion, now might be a great time for you to contact Rusty—he's even more enthusiastic about developing a GUI in sales after having seen the payroll operation.
>
> I look forward to working on a sales GUI after you meet with Rusty.

Hazel is neatly boxed into endorsing Niko's initiatives. The blind copy (bcc) to Rusty guarantees follow-through should Hazel fail to act. Boxing in takes planning, persistence, and skill, and Niko's clever use of this tactic distinguishes him as he intended.

Hazel also wins—she has been praised to the chairman and will profit from Niko's success. Likewise, Rusty, the head of payroll, and the company as a whole will all benefit. Niko has set up a favorable situation for all parties concerned.

## Avoiding the Box

> *The only way of catching a train I ever discovered is to miss the train before.*
>
> G. K. CHESTERTON

In win-win situations like Niko's, the players may be willing to accept a stacked deck. There are times, however, when you want the deck reshuffled—if it is not stacked in your favor. In particular, you must keep from being boxed in when dealing with a deck stacker who is known to set up win-lose situations.

*Scenario:* The company's objective is to have most of the employees schedule vacation time over the Christmas–New Year period when very little work gets done. As the company's pawn, the director of employee relations is told in no uncertain terms to make it happen. He decides that innocent-looking notices will box in a majority of employees who do not suspect that the company intends to tighten its standard operating procedures. The director is betting on the naivete of his employees and their natural tendency to procrastinate.

> January 2nd
>
> Corporate policy and tradition allow staff with a minimum of two years' seniority to select between a bonus based on annual profits (to be determined) and an extra week of vacation at a time subject to departmental schedules.
>
> Qualified staff are invited to make their selection on the bottom of this form, and sign, date, and return it to departmental supervisors by the end of the current week.
>
> Staff members who fail to respond on time may risk the loss of this benefit for the current calendar year, as unused vacation time cannot be carried over to the following year.

The opening announcement squeezes just a little. The following memo tightens the rules.

> March 1
>
> Qualified staff members who selected the option of an extra week of vacation time are encouraged to schedule their vacations during the first week of July, the first week of September, or the final week of December.

Catherine rejects the recommendation of dates and fills out the form to meet her own goals.

> 👍 Attached is your form, notarized by the department manager, scheduling my extra week's vacation for the second week of October.

The director of employee relations disregards this memo and proceeds with the plan of boxing in the staff.

> July 10
>
> Qualified staff members who opted for an extra week of vacation and have not yet scheduled this vacation time are cautioned that it

must be scheduled no later than the end of the current month. Otherwise, they may risk the loss of this benefit.

August 1

Due to the forthcoming inventory crunch, no extra weeks of vacation may be taken during the months of October or November. Any vacations scheduled for those months must be rescheduled no later than the 15th of the current month.

Catherine again refuses to be boxed in. The director's choice is reschedule it or lose it. Catherine counters with a choice of accept my decision or publicize your own deficiencies.

My extra week's vacation has been scheduled since the spring for the second week of October. The form was submitted on time and approved by my department manager.

My regular vacation is scheduled after that week, and so I will be out of the office October 7–28.

I cannot remake my plans to cover your rescheduling and will indeed be on vacation.

The employee relations director realizes that this and a few other exceptional cases aren't worth fighting over and focuses instead on the majority who offer no opposition.

December 1

Due to poor sales, the annual company bonus is expected to be considerably lower than usual this year. Thus, in a spirit of fairness, all qualified staff members who opted for the bonus are offered the opportunity to select the extra week of vacation to be taken during the final week of the current month. Those who wish to take advantage of this offer must do so in writing by the end of the current week.

We wish everyone a happy holiday season.

The trap is sprung, and all of the remaining players are boxed in.

# 13

# Uncorking Bottlenecks

*The direct assault of new ideas provokes a stubborn resistance, thus intensifying the difficulty of producing a change of outlook.*

B. H. LIDDELL HART

People become bottlenecks for productive and nonproductive reasons. A bottleneck might want to preserve the status quo to maintain quality or from personal laziness or fear of something new. Whatever the reason, a bottleneck is someone whose priorities differ from yours and who, as a result, slows down or blocks your progress.

## Meeting Their Priorities

*It pays to be obvious, especially if you have a reputation for subtlety.*

ISAAC ASIMOV

To loosen bottlenecks, find out what motivates them. Competent people who need information to do their jobs well often appear as bottlenecks. By recognizing this and meeting their needs, you may turn some bottlenecks into important allies.

*Scenario:* Rita is perceived as a bottleneck because she expects request forms to be complete before she'll act on them. By considering Rita's needs and taking the time to complete these forms, Beth may be able to convert this bottleneck into a supportive ally.

> To:      Rita
> From:   Beth
> I appreciate the time you took last week explaining the processing
> system, and I will be sure to forward the four forms in the future.
>    Thanks for the help and advice.

*Scenario:* Bullhead is perceived as a bottleneck because he expects to be
kept informed of every detail on each project in the office. Beth has
learned to keep Bullhead up to date with timely status reports that anticipate his questions and avert his bottleneck tendencies that would otherwise delay her progress.

> To:      Bullhead
> From:   Beth
> Attached is the status report on the Critical Co. order. I expect to
> have their purchase order on your desk for approval early next
> week.

There are times when you may need to appeal to corporate goals or a
sense of emergency to uncork a bottleneck, or when you must dislodge
the bottleneck by backing in to the problem.

*Scenario:* Beth has just received a rush order from the Critical Co. and is
aware that the paperwork to accompany the order is not complete. Knowing that Rita is likely to return the order for paperwork processing, she
appeals to Rita's sense of duty and adds a deadline—people who are stick-
lers for rules take deadlines seriously.

> To:      Rita
> From:   Beth
> Please process this order before the paperwork is complete—the
> company needs it to make the season's budget.
>    I'll stop by on my way to lunch to pick it up and to save you the
> trouble of having to deliver it.
>    Sorry for the missing form. This is an exceptional circumstance.

Alternatively, Beth could promote her case by overstating the situation
and its consequences, taking care to temper her exaggeration with reason:
remember the mink that cried "furrier" once too often.

> To:      Rita
> From:   Beth
> This is an emergency: we're processing a rush order for the Critical

Co., but we won't have the paperwork until Tuesday and we may lose both the order and the customer!

Please approve this requisition for cartons before the paperwork is complete. I'll stop by on my way to lunch to pick it up and to save you the trip of having to deliver it.

Beth could also back in to the more threatening issue by first introducing a more innocuous topic.

To:     Rita
From:   Beth

The computer, that paragon of efficiency, is dead. We were processing a rush order for the Critical Co. at the time and now we won't have the paperwork until Tuesday.

So that we don't lose the order and the customer (as well as the computer), please approve this order before the paperwork is complete. I'll stop by on my way to lunch to pick it up and to save you the trip of having to deliver it.

# Getting Their Attention

*The best way to get on in the world is to make people believe it's to their advantage to help you.*

JEAN DE LA BRUYERE

When bottlenecks are more attentive to the letter than the spirit of corporate productivity, you are challenged to find ways to attract their attention and redirect their priorities to more closely match your own. You may gain the bottleneck's attention by flattery, by being perceived as an ally, or by stacking the deck.

Flattery can be an effective way to penetrate the bottleneck's guard: no one ever seems too busy to accept a compliment. Excessive praise or flattery is often recognizable as insincere, but who among us is invulnerable to expressions of esteem?

To:     H. Heine
From:   Hugh Sharif

The defense you conducted against the *Miranda* litigation was certainly on track.

I hear we might have been in serious trouble if you hadn't come up with that precedent from *Diogenes vs Phaedrus*. Brilliant concept!

Heine is probably nodding in agreement, flattered that someone as perceptive as Hugh is taking the time to express his admiration in so accurate and tasteful a manner.

Having played his way up to the net, it's time for Hugh to earn the point.

> I hope you won't think it impertinent of me to ask if you could now turn your attention to the *Chelsea* case, on which I need your determination.

An indirect compliment may magnify its effect. Most of us like to be recognized for our accomplishments; and praise received through a third-party carries a special aura.

> To:    Ms. Finch
> From:  Hugh Sharif
>
> The defense that Hank Heine conducted against the *Miranda* litigation was certainly on track. I understand we might have been in serious trouble if he hadn't come up with that precedent from *Diogenes vs Phaedrus*—a brilliant concept.
>      I could learn a lot from someone with Heine's experience. Perhaps I'll get a chance to assist him on one of his cases sometime this year.

There is no guarantee that Finch will share Hugh's praise with Heine, but Hugh could share it directly under a cover memo:

> To:    H. Heine
> From:  Hugh Sharif
>
> I thought you'd want to see the note I recently sent Finch.
>      By the way, I really do need your determination on the *Chelsea* case now.

You may be able to clear a bottleneck by selling yourself as an ally—by helping the bottleneck look good or giving him credit he may not have received elsewhere.

*Scenario:* Heine, the company lawyer, delays decisions with phrases like "We'll have to think more about this before coming to a decision." Felicia is three months pregnant and wants a flextime policy for mothers. She suspects that Heine is against the plan, which would be defeated without his support. Her strategy is to infiltrate his defenses and then wear him down.

> To:     Mr. Heine
> From:   Felicia Santiago
>
> It seems that the flextime plan is moving ahead too quickly. As an employee who may be affected by it someday, I feel it is much too early for the company to come to a decision. We really should explore it further, don't you agree?

By appearing to oppose passage of this policy in its current form, Felicia loses nothing and appeals to Heine's cautious nature. If she can convince Heine that she may be useful to him, she may be able to get a flextime policy approved in time for her own use.

When time is running short and you need a quick score, you may be able to stack the deck against a bottleneck. As with other aggressive tactics, this one is risky—it may force your targets into hardening their resolve or counterattacking you. So temper your approach—a reasonably friendly relationship may make your objective more obtainable.

*Scenario:* When Jack was promoted, no cubicle appropriate to his new position was available. One will become vacant next month, but Jack suspects that Mr. Bullhead intends to leave him where he is and give the space to an incoming staff member.

A meek E-mail request from Jack is easily ignored.

 Bill—

> People have been asking why I haven't moved into a cubicle in keeping with my recent upgrade. I've been reminding them that you're the man in charge, and that you'll surely get to it as soon as possible.
>
>     Is there one available?
>
> —Jack

A more forceful argument is also weak if it requires an answer from Bullhead, who is known to ignore his E-mail for days at a time.

 Bill—

> I've been looking for an opportunity to set up the printer I got after my promotion. Since I do a lot of printing, this would sure save me a lot of back-and-forth time.

> It would also make everybody else who uses the common printer very happy. Isn't the cubicle that Murayama is moving out of available?
>
> —Jack

Fortunately, Jack has just read the chapter on Stacking the Deck, enabling him to compose a more compelling memo to coerce the office manager into assigning him the cubicle.

 Bill—

> I just heard that cubicle B–313 is about to become available. It is the right size for the new printer and it matches my grade level.
> My using it would have the following benefits:
>
> 1. It is central to those people who need access to the printer.
>
> 2. It is nearer your office and would facilitate communication between us.
>
> 3. It is consistent with your concern that everyone be treated according to the rules.
>
> As Friday is a half day (due to the holidays), I'll move after work if that's okay with you.
>
> —Jack

Of course, this bold approach might backfire by getting Bullhead angry, but the worst he's likely to do is turn Jack down. Though a strained relationship with the office manager may be inconvenient, sometimes the stakes are worth the risk.

# 14

## Team Play

*Then join hand in hand, brave Americans all!*
*By uniting we stand, by dividing we fall.*

JOHN DICKINSON

An effective team is a structure that focuses the talents of its participants. Team members cooperate when they expect the payoff to be greater than the rewards that are likely to result from an equal individual effort. When people join a team, they don't lose their individuality—in fact, the strengths, weaknesses, and idiosyncrasies of the players often are magnified. A skillful player can capitalize on the diversity and compensate for individual weaknesses.

Successful team performance requires the same elements as other business performance: commitment to a goal, action to advance the plan, follow through on the details, and consolidation of results.

## Shaping Team Commitment

*Many a man gets to the top of the ladder and then finds*
*that it has been leaning against the wrong wall.*

LAURENCE J. PETER

Without goals, we risk gaining something we don't really want, overlooking something worthwhile, or failing to recognize the value of something already achieved. Goals may evolve as we work toward them, but if they are developed by the team—rather than imposed—the agenda is more likely to be realistic. Team members who set their own goals tend to stay committed to them.

*Scenario:* Generic Concepts, Inc., is a prominent manufacturer of condoms. The Marketing department is about to conclude its five-year plan and is experiencing difficulties in adopting a new plan. The tension extends to the Advertising department, where Frank is trying to get the company unstuck. He realizes that the diversity in his department may result in people working at cross-purposes, so he surveys the group to see if they can identify a common goal.

> To:     Alan, Bob, Carl, Danielle, Elizabeth
> From:   Frank
> Re:     Marketing Plan
> We've about completed the current five-year marketing plan, and I,
> for one, am concerned about potential revisions.
> Have you any thoughts about these next five years?

Their responses run from aggressive to conservative. Alan thinks the ads must be more upscale: "The people most likely to get turned off are no longer potential customers." Bob believes "it's our duty and opportunity to educate the public about the safety benefits of our products." Carl is concerned about "offending millions of people who aren't used to having sex rubbed in their noses in the media." Danielle emphasizes the importance of advertising personal products "as tastefully as possible." Elizabeth eyes the competition: "If Old's Rubber or some other company comes up with a major theme before we do, we'll be playing catch-up forever."

This feedback offers Frank insight into each of his colleagues, enabling him to initiate a plan. He probes even further with memos like the following.

> To:     Alan
> From:   Frank
> Re:     New Marketing Plan
> Assuming you were able to create an upscale marketing plan to air
> on MTV, what problems do you foresee in presenting this plan to
> the company?

The results of his informal survey convince Frank that the Advertising department lacks leadership and focus. The members are riding off in all directions, so he tries focusing the group toward a common goal.

> To:     Alan, Bob, Carl, Danielle, Elizabeth
> From:   Frank
> Each of you has expressed concern about our marketing plan—

I think we all have concerns about the future, although for very different reasons.

Can we get together Friday morning at 9 in the conference room to discuss this?

Should the meeting bomb, Frank can disclaim any ulterior motive. If successful, the meeting may lead seamlessly to his campaign.

# Sustaining the Team

*Never tell people how to do things. Tell them what to do, and they will surprise you with their ingenuity.*

GEN. GEORGE S. PATTON

Members of a team perform best when they feel included and associate the team cause with *their* cause. In an ideal world, each player makes a special effort to include and support the other team members. In the real world, however, leaderless groups tend to drift apart without approaching consensus unless someone assumes de facto leadership.

*Scenario:* As the meeting progresses, Frank remains unobtrusively supportive of each member. Eventually he breaks into the discussion with a simple summary: "We've been talking about these issues in detail. Now seems a good time to end the discussion and start thinking about each other's points of view."

Shortly after the meeting and before an alternative leader emerges, Frank starts to formulate team goals that include the entire group.

To:     Alan, Bob, Carl, Danielle, Elizabeth
From:   Frank

We are all concerned about what management will decree as a five-year plan—after all, if the six of us professionals have such divergent points of view, think what the people upstairs might impose.

It's apparent that we have some important areas of agreement:

- The six of us are committed to the industry, the company, and our jobs.

- We all agree with Elizabeth that the industry is on the cusp of change, and change means opportunity.

> It's also obvious that we need more information, to which end I'd
> like to propose five teams (see attached), each with its own area. I'll
> work on *intergroup communications* as a member of each team.

Frank solidifies his leadership with a series of personal memos. These
employ a variety of sweeteners to ensure that each member recognizes
his or her membership in the group. Frank knows that encouragement
and acknowledgment are hard to resist.

> To:    Elizabeth
> From:  Frank
> I teamed you with Carl on the question of our competition because
> this is your prime interest and an area where we all defer to you.
> Don't forget to sell Carl on the ramifications of doing nothing while
> Old's Rubber steals a march on us.
>      You and Danielle have the most realistic view of what our future
> customers might find acceptable or unacceptable, so you're teamed
> on this topic. You should be able to convert both the radicals and
> conservatives among us.

A limitation or shortcoming can be turned into an advantage. For
example, you might call a reactionary "traditional," a plodder "thorough," or an off-the-cuff notion "fresh." Frank uses this technique to
remind Bob to be tactful when presenting his findings to the group.

> To:    Bob
> From:  Frank
> You have the strongest social conscience of us all, which is why I
> teamed you with Danielle on the profile of our customers in the next
> five years, and with Alan on what the correct pitch should be.
>      I understand your concern about safe sex as an AIDS preventive,
> but please remember that some team members are not as aware as
> you. Unless you discover reasons to modify this recommendation,
> could you phrase this concept as "protecting your health"? This
> would include all health-related functions of condoms without
> needlessly rattling members of our team.

One way to minimize your indebtedness is to keep the score even—
offer something in exchange for what you want.

> To:    Danielle
> From:  Frank
> You're teamed with Bob on the nature of our customers over the

next five years.  My personal opinion is that our group consciousness is pretty much in accord, *but* that we will not be able to get any plan through that uses the word AIDS in a prominent manner.  I'd appreciate your trying to tone Bob down on this point.

In appreciation of your help, I also put you on our future customers' definition of acceptability (with Liz).  This is an area of interest to you, and you both have realistic views on the topic.

Don't forget, you have to convert all of us—radicals and conservatives alike!

Problem solving is an effective motivator.  Most people will exert the effort to solve a problem that is presented as a challenge.

To:     Alan
From:  Frank

I teamed you with Carl on the question of our customers' profile because everything hinges on that point.

Al, I don't need to tell you that Carl is too demanding to accept fog like "upscale" or assumptions that "those who would be put off no longer use our products."  We need real substance here.

I believe that Carl, while tough, is fair.  If anyone can persuade him, you can.  Please pull out the stops and sell for all of us on the team!

Market your idea by appealing to people's self-interest.  Offer them what you think *they* think is best for them and you're likely to register the sale.

To:     Carl
From:  Frank

As our senior, you are strongly oriented toward our current and historic channels/competition.  We put you on future marketing channels (with Alan) and competition (with Elizabeth) because of your knowledge of channels and how they work both for and against the competition.

Assuming we can reach a consensus and our recommendations are accepted on high, we will need a workable means of channeling our message to compete against Old's Rubber.  This is where we need you most of all!

Good luck!

# Channeling the Team

*There go my people. I must find out where they are*
*going so I can lead them.*

ALEXANDRE LEDRU-ROLLIN

Maintaining momentum is critical to any common effort. For both team leaders and members, this means providing a supportive atmosphere, helping people adhere to the evolving team goals, and following up on all activities. A brief clarification, timely reminder, or thank you creates good will and reinforces the team's commitment. Consistent follow-ups can also preclude future misunderstandings.

Team members benefit when interactions among them are personable. Forwarding an article of interest to another team member can rekindle a sense of camaraderie.

> To:    Carl
> From:  Frank
> I recall your daughter is planning to attend a school back east.
> Thought this map of New England wineries would be of interest.

Team goals are always evolving, and team members must be able to redirect players away from unproductive tangents.

> To:    Bob
> From:  Frank
> I agree with your observations on the direction that our society is taking, and the real versus ideal role that Generic could play in this society. Thank you for sharing your concerns with me.
>
> These considerations must be reflected in the marketing plan we develop. However, we each have a personal perspective and it would be counterproductive to get into a *team* discussion of these concerns.
>
> You and Danielle are investigating our market profile. I'm sure these concerns will be reflected in this profile. The team (and the company) can then see the actuality rather than simply listen to the philosophy.

Courtesy is easily integrated with team activities. For instance, a tactful thank you note can facilitate your pursuit of an objective.

> To:      Elizabeth
> From:    Frank
>
> Enjoyed the game with you last Saturday.  Next week I may be able
> to handle that uncanny backhand of yours.
>     On a different topic, have you had any success with determining
> the marketing plans at Old's Rubber?

In dealing with peers, a casual approach to instruction is preferable to
a more officious tone.  At Generic, Frank requested input from Alan on
marketing channels, but he received only a few notes amounting to
unsubstantiated conclusions.  To obtain an improved report, Frank
refers to Alan's report as "interim notes," encouraging Alan to complete the task.

> To:      Alan
> From:    Frank
> Re:      Your interim notes on channels
>
> Thanks for sharing your notes.  You are on the right track, and this is
> a great start.
>     What "underground papers" are you including, and what type of
> cost/circulation is involved?

A successful team needs to share information, most of which may be
easily conveyed by memo.  However, too much information—or information that is outside the interest of the team—can cause disruption and
redirection.  In such situations, direct the team's attention to the most
closely related issues.

> To:      Alan, Bob, and Danielle
> cc:      Carl and Elizabeth
> From:    Frank
> Re:      Progress on Team Effort—Competition
>
> Carl and Elizabeth have interviewed people at Old's Rubber and
> have obtained some information on their plans and copies of their
> Annual Report.  Copies of both are attached FYI.
>     Note that Old's is on a similar track to ours (paragraph 2).  If we
> want to be first with the best proposal, we certainly have our work
> cut out.
>     On the other hand, I think that this shows we are on the right
> track!

# Rewarding the Team

*I shan't be pulling the levers there but I shall be a very*
*good back-seat driver.*

MARGARET THATCHER

A successful team leader recognizes the contributions of individual team members and shares the reward with them. It is to everyone's benefit that credit is apportioned fairly. Often a challenge to leadership is launched just as the goal comes into sight, a power grab that can disrupt the team. Taking credit for the work of others is like trying to join the bandwagon as the conductor.

> To: Alan, Bob, Danielle, Elizabeth, Frank
> From: Carl
> Re: Announcement of New Marketing Plan
>
> As the senior member of the Advertising department, I plan to make the announcement of the recommendations that we have discussed.

Frank firmly stops Carl's attempt to usurp the leadership role with candor, an appeal to Carl's self-interest, and support from team members. The team members support Frank on this, recognizing his contribution to the team and trusting him to share the rewards fairly.

> To: Carl
> From: Frank
>
> It would be counterproductive for you to announce our results for three major reasons:
>
> 1. Your previously held position on the sensitivities of the market is well known throughout the organization and would negatively impact on the effect of the entire report.
>
> 2. By presenting the report, you would not be able to take full credit for your contributions on competition and marketing channels.
>
> 3. Alan, Bob, Danielle, and Elizabeth all agree that, having

participated on each of the teams, I am in the position to best represent all of our contributions.

I'll be writing the cover memo tomorrow morning. Could you be available to review it with me?

When possible, announce a victory with full deference and recognition to all the participants—these same collaborators may again play on your team.

The team Frank put together has created a marketing plan and written a report. Frank coordinates the report and prepares a cover memo that includes each participant's contribution to the department's plan. Like a triumphant pirate, Frank spreads the plunder among the members of his crew.

> To:      Marketing and Advertising Management
> cc:      Alan, Bob, Carl, Danielle, Elizabeth
> From:   Frank
> Re:      Attached Recommendations
>
> As the existing five-year marketing plan has run its course, the Advertising department has put together recommendations for a new five-year plan.
>      This has been a real team effort with the added benefit of welding together a cohesive resource to confront the future.
>      Our report addresses:
>
> * Our customers over the next five years
> * The competition
> * Marketing channels needed to reach this market
> * The personal preferences of this market
> * The slant that our promotion should take.

Now Frank has an opportunity to decide where and how to submit the plan. If he submits it, with or without a cover memo, *only* to his boss Sandy, the head of Advertising, Sandy will probably write a separate cover memo to assume credit before passing the report along to Marketing.

If he sends a cover memo and the report *only* to the director of Marketing, a more senior position, Sandy will be offended at Frank's having gone over Sandy's head.

If he submits the report with a cover memo addressed to *both* directors, Sandy can share reflected glory but not snatch all the credit.

The choice is obvious: Frank sends the report and cover memo to the two directors, ending with a line of kudos for his boss:

> We are grateful to the Director of Advertising for providing an environment where independent thought can flourish.

# 15

# Penetrating the Crack
# in the Clouds

*Strike before the iron cools.*

A. SMITH

The apprentice system of the last century was harsh but provided people entering the workforce with skills and security. Apprenticeship was displaced by company towns, then unions, followed by paternal corporations. Each afforded the worker opportunities for learning and for earning security.

In our modern workplace, you must provide your own opportunities for learning or earning. Management hides in the clouds and leaves you in the shadows. When a crack in the clouds does occur, make sure you are ready to take advantage of the opportunity.

In the short term, your survival in the corporate environment will be supported by the tactics in the first fourteen chapters of *Manipulative Memos*. This respite will enable you to plan your long-term career goals and prepare to penetrate the crack in the clouds.

Comfortable in the reinforced security of your position, you will more easily recognize opportunities to force a crack in the clouds through your own affiliations, further education, and networks. You will cultivate mentors, increase your control over your own environment, and remain alert for the chance to apply your newly acquired arsenal of manipulative skills.

With your environment and your career under control, you will be able to bask in the sunshine of a brighter career path.

# Surviving

*In preparing for battle, I have always found that plans are useless, but planning is indispensable.*

DWIGHT D. EISENHOWER

Personal and positional survival hinge on understanding your *relative* place within your company. On a positional level, consider whether your department or position enjoys any special protection from on high. How does its profitability compare with that of other departments—too low will dissatisfy decision makers, too high may lead to envy and takeover. Are many of your functions duplicated elsewhere: could you be pruned or merged?

On a personal level, evaluate your status relative to your peers. Are you associated with productivity or considered among the brightest of the Young Turks? Do you have a specialized skill? Are you the best memo writer in the entire organization?

By reviewing your goals, your strengths, and your weaknesses, you can plan your path to survival. Only by surviving can you go on to the next step—penetrating the crack in the clouds.

An important aspect of surviving is to maintain good working relationships with colleagues and those who can protect you.

*Scenario:* Tina Upman is no longer subservient to I. B. Grabbe, although he continues to try to regain reporting control over her. Tina strengthens her position when Finch, the CFO, compliments her for her rapid rise through the ranks of finance. Tina recognizes an opportunity and seizes it.

> To:     Ms. Finch, CFO
> From:   Tina Upman, Associate Chief, Budget
>
> Thank you for your kind words during our brief conversation yesterday. It is gratifying to be appreciated.
>
> Although not everyone here shares your views on this issue, it is clear that a promising career path is open to any woman in this company who is willing to make the effort. I can't help wondering what it was like before you were in charge.
>
> Again, I enjoyed meeting you and hope that I continue to justify your confidence.

Under the guise of a polite follow-up, Tina seeks to open a path to a powerful decision maker. Her suggestions that some people may be less supportive of women and that Finch herself might be responsible for having opened doors in this direction invite continued conversation. Finch may or may not respond, but Tina feels confident that she can now correspond directly with the CFO on any topic remotely related to women's issues in the workplace.

# Thriving

*Don't be afraid to take a big step. You can't cross a chasm in two small jumps.*

DAVID LLOYD GEORGE

The best way to prepare for the future is to continue your education, actively network, and maintain your mobility. These activities can improve a promising career path or help you take unpleasant realities in stride.

## Education

*Education is learning what you didn't even know you didn't know.*

DANIEL J. BOORSTIN

Managers commonly view further study as an indication of enthusiasm, hard work, and motivation, and they consider these characteristics when evaluating staff for promotion. The *act* of taking a course is often more important than the *content* of the course. Many companies have educational reimbursement programs through which you might enroll in courses with relevance to *future* positions.

*Scenario:* Finch mentioned to Tina Upman that a course in budget forecasting and analysis was being offered as part of City University's evening program. If Tina wants to hitch her star to Finch, she will enroll in the recommended class. Even if she takes a loan to pay for it, she'll get her money's worth in increased power at work. As an immediate benefit, she gains recognition from her boss by borrowing leverage from the CFO.

To:     Mr. O'Boile, Deputy Controller
cc:     R. Finch
From:  Tina Upman

I have enrolled in City University's budget forecasting and analysis course recommended to me by Ms. Finch for the spring semester.
    Although I'll be leaving the office early on Tuesdays and Thursdays, I will not fall behind on my work.

Of course, she lets Finch know that she has acted on the suggestion.

To:     Ms. Finch, CFO
From:  Tina Upman

Thank you so much for your thoughtful suggestion about the budget forecasting and analysis course. I have enrolled for the spring semester and will have no trouble fitting it into my schedule.

Tina follows up periodically to keep lines of communication open with Finch.

To:     Ms. Finch, CFO
From:  Tina Upman

The budget forecasting and analysis course you recommended is great! The professor is Dr. Algorithm, and he is helping me do some special applications for the company.

At the end of the course, Tina continues the dialogue by applying the course to an area of mutual interest.

To:     Ms. Finch, CFO
From:  Tina Upman

I have successfully completed the budget forecasting and analysis course. It reinforced a number of principles with which I was already familiar and introduced some new ideas as well.
    I am attaching a *draft* proposal in computerized cost control for our company and would like to discuss this with you further.
    I'll call next Tuesday to set a date.

Following a weekend seminar, also recommended by Finch, and several conversations with her, Tina is now responsible for a quarterly report and two staff members formerly supervised by Finch. She is an asset to Finch, respected by O'Boile, safe from Grabbe's clutches, and on an ascending track.

## Networking

> *Opportunity is missed by most people because it is*
> *dressed in overalls and looks like work.*

THOMAS EDISON

Successful people generally maintain a large number of contacts. The spice in networking is the diversity of pursuits and talents people bring one another. The common element for members of a network is that they are supportive of each other.

*Scenario:* Frank is an effective networker. He provides the monthly agenda for his professional organization and a local service group. At meetings, he trades stock tips, new jokes, mystery novels, and the fact that he is looking for a used car. He also practices his oratory skills.

Frank has set a goal of moving from advertising into market management. The most direct way of achieving this goal is to approach the marketing director of his company.

> To:     M. Mystique, Marketing Director
> From:   Frank
>
> I have been taking market management courses and know that my talents and interests lie in that direction.
>     I would therefore like to meet with you for lunch, at your convenience, and seek your views on making this change to marketing.

Frank calls on the president of his civic group to lend assistance.

> Kenny—
>
> I am currently in advertising and want to switch over to market management. I am taking several related courses with the intention of getting hired as an assistant market manager by a large marketer of consumer products.
>     Any ideas?
>
> —Frank
> P.S. See you Thursday and I'll bring copies of the agenda with me.

Another obvious networking possibility is with the competition—in this case, the teacher of his forthcoming class.

To:     Jon Fastrack
From:   Frank
Dear Mr. Fastrack:

I will be taking your course on market management and wanted to let you know up front that I am an employee of one of your competitors (Generic). As I am in advertising, I see no conflict of interest.

My purpose in taking your course is twofold: to prepare for a career move toward market management in the future and to meet our industry's famous Jon Fastrack.

I look forward to meeting you and learning from you next week.

## Mobility

*There are no shortcuts to anyplace worth going.*

BEVERLY SILLS

Survival in corporate America demands mobility. It may be upward, following in your boss's wake; laterally to another department, if you attract the notice of a stronger manager or discover a better career path; or outward, by moving to another company. Before you move, however, determine if your chances of survival are improved by the move—if your new position is secure or vulnerable to pruning and if your reputation is likely to transfer with you.

The answers to these questions helped Frank make an intelligent decision, as announced by the following memo.

To:     Staff
From:   Jon Fastrack
Re:     Marketing Staff

I am pleased to announce a new addition to our group.

Tina, on the other hand, moved up another notch on the same ladder.

To:     Finance Staff
From:   B. B. O'Boile, Deputy Controller

I am pleased to announce the promotion of Ms. Tina Upman to the newly created position of Adjunct Deputy Controller. Ms. Upman will continue to report to me on budget issues and to Ms. Finch on analysis issues. I. B. Grabbe, who formerly reported to me, will now report to Ms. Upman.

# Basking in the Sun

*Those who know how to win are much more numerous than those who know how to make proper use of their victories.*

POLYBIUS

When you control your environment, the sun illuminates your life. This is true whether you are oriented to success, winning, or self-realization.

In the Olympic games, the gold medal signifies the highest achievable standard. To a few competitors, winning the silver medal means failing to gain the gold. To most, however, even the bronze would crown the efforts of a lifetime. Winning isn't limited to coming in first. If it were, then only two high-jumpers—one male and one female—would succeed every four years and all their competitors would be doomed to failure.

The sun shines on those who make progress toward their goals—jumping higher than before, earning a promotion, gaining the respect of friends and colleagues, or feeling more in control. Such achievements allow you to bask in the sunshine, brightening your career, and making you feel better about yourself.

Assess your circumstances, make and pursue opportunities, acquire mentors, and avoid burning bridges—a timely and persuasive memo can open paths and dissipate the thickest clouds. Why hope for better weather when, with creativity and practice, you can control it?

# Sources

Brockway, Wallace, editor. *A Treasury of the World's Great Letters.* Simon & Schuster, 1941.

Carpenter, Donna Sammons, and John Feloni. *The Fall of the House of Hutton.* Harper & Row, 1992.

Clurman, Richard M. *To the End of Time.* Simon & Schuster, 1992.

Lathrop, Richard. *Who's Hiring Who.* Ten Speed, 1977.

North, Oliver L., and William Novak. *Under Fire.* HarperCollins, 1991.

Rosenberg, Arthur D., and David V. Hizer. *The Resume Handbook, Second Edition.* Bob Adams, Inc., 1990.

Schuster, Max Lincoln, editor. *A Treasury of the World's Great Letters.* Simon & Schuster, 1960.

Sifakis, Carl. *The Mafia Encyclopedia.* Facts on File, 1987.

Tepper, Ron. *The Only 250 Letters & Memos Managers Will Ever Need.* John Wiley & Sons, 1990.

Wilson, Colin. *Rasputin and the Fall of the Romanovs.* Arthur Barker, Ltd., 1964.

Winnick, R. H., editor. *Letters of Archibald MacLeish.* Houghton Mifflin Co., 1983.

# Index

The earth is the center, the sun, moon and stars revolve around the earth. —Pt

It's flat surrounded by a big wall —Cosmas

memo

Property of Alexandrian Library

The evolution